Building Block Quilts

by Sara Nephew

Dedication

To my children, Elizabeth, Derek and Alexander

Acknowledgements

Special thanks to all the talented quilters who helped piece samples for this book: Annette Austin, Joan Hanson, Laura Reinstatler, Elizabeth Sevy and Laurie Vilbrandt.

Special thanks to Charisa Anderson for sharing her wonderful "Paint-box" design.

Credits

Photography by Carl Murray
Graphics by Jean Streinz

Building Block Quilts

Clearview Triangle

8311 180th St. S.E.
Snohomish, WA 98290

Library of Congress Card Number 89-82476
ISBN 0-9621172-1-8

Contents

Preface

The 60° triangle is my favorite shape. A special characteristic of this triangle and its variations is that it is able to produce a 3-dimensional effect. One familiar quilt that uses this effect is TUMBLING BLOCK, or BABY BLOCK. Architects and draftsmen also use these 60°, 30°, and 120° angles to create a 3-D illusion in drawings of buildings, machine parts, etc. This is called isometric drawing.

But don't let this talk about angles and architecture make you nervous. This is not a technical book. You don't need to know math or have any drafting skills.

Any quilter can use rotary cutting and speed piecing techniques and follow one of the patterns in this book to produce a quilt with a 3-D look. Or you can try the methods and suggestions given here to design an original pattern.

Even the smallest step into the world of *Building Block Quilts* can produce big gains in one's ability to handle values, colors and angles. Learning something new multiplies self-confidence. And, best of all, making a 3-D quilt is fun.

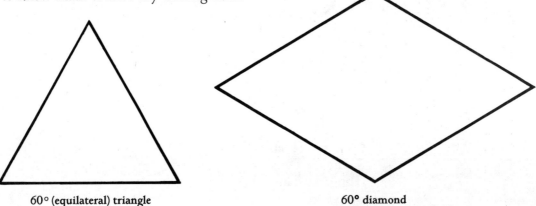

60° (equilateral) triangle   60° diamond

Introduction

This book is organized as a workbook. In the first section, a small amount of 3-D theory is given so the quilter will understand the underlying principles of these patterns. Information about choosing fabric colors and values is also included to help make the quilts more impressively 3-D.

Next the tools are described and then rotary cutting and speed piecing techniques are given. These are the same time-saving cutting directions as those in my previous book, as the methods haven't changed. One or two new items have been added, however, since I continue to learn. Changing the aim and approach to color and value, even while cutting some of the same basic

shapes, produces entirely different kinds of quilts.

Then, in the pages that follow, a step-by-step pattern section gives directions for 14 exciting Building Block quilts. Some of these patterns are traditional designs, and some are original quilts. Last, some additional information on designing quilts may suggest new approaches to the interested quilter.

It is best to read through at least the front section of the book (up to the patterns) before beginning to piece a particular quilt. If the cutting methods are familiar, the information on 3-D effects will help you apply the methods to this new kind of quilt. Then choose a pattern and quilt in a new dimension!

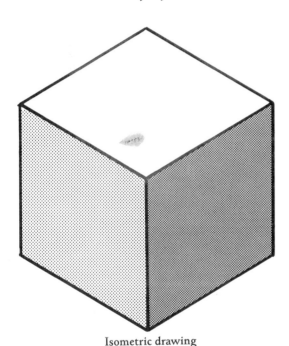

Artistic perspective

Isometric drawing

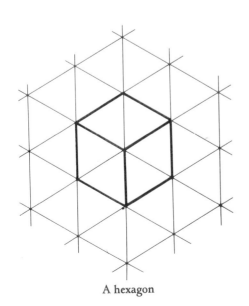

A hexagon

The Shapes of 3-D

Most quilters are familiar with at least one 60° 3-D pattern. TUMBLING BLOCK is a traditional pattern that has always intrigued quilters with its dimensional possibilities. Other 60° patterns have been used by quilters, like STARS AND BLOCKS, or ECCLE-SIASTICAL. To understand why these patterns have a 3-D look, a brief discussion of theory will be helpful.

There are two ways to draw a shape or scene that seems to have three dimensions (length, width, and depth). The first method is called true perspective or artistic perspective. A dot is placed somewhere on the page (vanishing point) and lines running from the foreground to the vanishing point determine the shape of the object drawn. Objects thus appear the way our eye actually sees them, larger in the parts that are close to us and smaller in the parts that are farther away. This results in many different shapes and angles being drawn. To make a quilt from this drawing, a template must be constructed for each separate shape shown in the drawing, a time-consuming process that does not appeal to many quilters. Of course, beautiful and impressive quilts can result.

The second way to line-draw a three-dimensional object is called isometric drawing. Instead of unlimited angles, only 30°, 60°, and 120° angles are drawn. This means that the number of shapes that will be drawn is limited also. These shapes are used in many familiar quilt designs.

An architect uses drafting tools to create 60° 3-D shapes. We can use equilateral graph paper to short circuit a lot of work. Underlying all isometric design is a grid of equilateral triangles. On this grid, lines and shapes can be drawn and these outlines can be colored in to produce many flat designs familiar to quilters, like GRANDMOTHER'S FLOWER GARDEN or SIX-POINTED STAR. Or they can be shaded in such a way that an illusion of depth is instantly created.

For example: a hexagon is drawn on equilateral graph paper. Lines are added to divide this shape into planes (flat surfaces). Then the three planes created are shaded in light, medium, and dark to enhance the illusion of a cube. This cube is constructed from three 60° diamonds, all the same size, so one template could be constructed that could be used by a quilter to produce many cubes. This is an indication of how important this 3-D approach could be to quilters.

Any shape or series of shapes that can be drawn on equilateral graph paper can be shaded to produce a 3-D look. Sometimes a few additional lines must be added. Put outlines on a whole page and shade it, and a quilt design is created.

3-D Rules

A few rules will help shading to be more effectively 3-D.

1. Choose a consistent light source. The simplest way to do this is to imagine a lamp shining on the pattern outline. The light side of the shape has the lamp shining directly on it. The dark side of the shape has no light falling on it, because it's directly opposite the lamp, and the medium colored sides are in between.

2. Choose colors that are clearly dark, medium and light, so the shapes and planes are distinct from each other. More about color choices below.

3. Nature places our light source above, so often this is a good choice to help designs "read" 3-D.

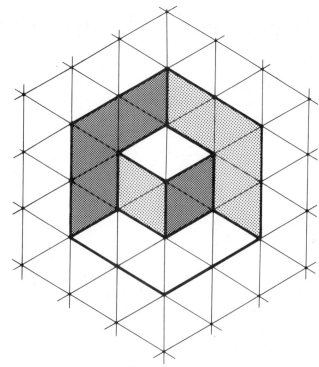

Shaded—a small hexagon inside a larger one

Using Fabric to Shade a 3-D Shape

There are two ways of using fabric to shade a 3-D shape.

1. Strips can be cut from a range of values and sewed together in order from light to dark to achieve **graded shading** of one part of the 3-D shape. This set of strips, or strata, should be planned to be the right size with seam allowances, etc. The piece desired can be drawn on scratch paper to size, strips of color sketched in, and then number of strips, width of strip plus seam allowance, etc., will not be too difficult to calculate. Stick to simple measurements that add up to the strip width necessary for cutting the shape desired, adding seam allowances inside the shape as necessary.

2. Or one piece can be cut as a color unit from light, medium or dark fabric. Many traditional 3-D quilts are done this way.

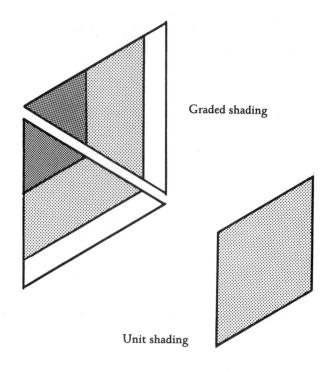

Graded shading

Unit shading

Choosing Fabrics for a Building Block Quilt

Color

The most important quality of color when designing for depth is **value**. This term describes the darkness or lightness of a color. One way to see the value of a color in comparison to others is to squint. This reduces the amount of light entering the eye, and the effect is one of evening-at-will, with all color shades being somewhat reduced to shades of gray.

Many 3-D designs require colors in three values: light, medium and dark. A slightly more difficult assignment is a design that has a background, thus requiring light, medium, dark and a background color that stands out from the other colors.

There are a number of ways to help the background remain distinct from the foreground of the design. All of the color values in the foreground could be moved toward lighter colors, and then the background made dark. Or all the foreground could be moved toward darker colors, and the background made light. Another alternative is to use a distinctly different color in the foreground (for example, if the design were all in shades of red, and the background green). Or a scene printed on fabric could be behind the 3-D geometry of the quilt design.

Some interesting effects can be obtained with a quilt's background. A place to begin when designing the background would be to decide if you want a flat background (all one color) or a graded background. A graded background could progress from light to dark, perhaps from the center out or from one side, either in reverse of the way the blocks are shaded or so as to emphasize the impression of a light source at one side. The more that is learned about how to incorporate and direct the visual impressions of light in the quilt design, the more creative background choices can be.

Of course, as well as choosing colors in the **values** desired, a pleasing color combination is preferred. You are probably familiar with the classic color schemes:

1. The **monochromatic** (one-color) design is easy to use in a 3-D quilt, since it narrows the choice to light, medium and dark values. Other than that, the appeal of the large or small prints or slight changes in hue or intensity are the only considerations. Work with one color in its whole range of shades and tints as well as black and white. For example, red goes from the very lightest pink all the way to the darkest maroon.

2. **Complementary** colors are opposite each other on the color wheel. Red and green, blue and orange, purple and yellow, are the simplest complementary color schemes. Then choose dark, medium and light from these colors.

3. **Analogous** color schemes use colors related to each other on one side of the color wheel. Orange, red, magenta and purple are all in line along the red side of the color wheel.

Any combination of colors can be used as long as dark, medium and light values are emphasized in the design. Special care must be taken with the inherent intensity or warmth of certain colors. Some colors radiate and some colors recede. For example, a hand-dyed packet of various shades of yellow probably needs to be considered all light colors. Many intense reds also come forward to the eye.

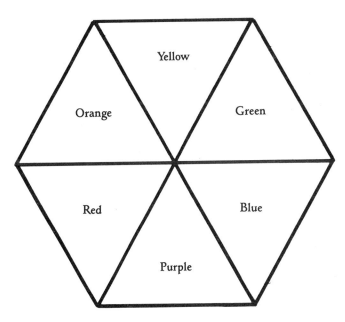

See "Paintbox"...a Quiltmakers colorwheel on page 52

Fabrics to Use

Prints can be wonderfully effective in a 3-D pattern. Almost anything goes. Small prints and solids are easy to work with. Large prints sometimes are more difficult to assign a value to, since cutting breaks the pattern so much. Safest choices are large prints where the foreground of the print is almost the same value as the background. Limiting use of a large print to one value of the design may be wise. HONEYCOMB WAFFLE on pg. 32 is an example of the stunning results that can be obtained when a large print (in this case, hand-dyed) is used successfully.

A heightened sense of dimension can be achieved by the use of stripes and plaids, since these surface lines help to define the flat planes of the shape. BOX OF TRICKS, shown in color on page 35, was pieced entirely of fabrics from Roberta Horton's "Lines" collection and "Heritage Homespun II." The woven patterns impart a mellow old-fashioned look as well as an increased illusion of depth.

All of the patterns in this book have yardage requirements for light, medium and dark fabrics. These could be just three colors purchased at a fabric store. These choices could also be enriched by dividing each value into more than one fabric. So instead of just choosing one red fabric as the medium color, the quilter might choose 3 different reds, or even 3 different medium colors, perhaps a red, a blue, and a fuchsia.

Carrying this technique even further results in a scrap quilt, where many different fabrics are used. 3-D designs are often effective as scrap quilts. STRIP CITY, shown on page 34, mixes modern fabrics with a wide range of remnants from my shelves.

A good way to begin choosing fabric from your own collection for a 3-D scrap quilt is to start three piles of fabrics. In front of the place for each pile lay a swatch of a cool (blue or gray are good) color in the value desired—light, medium or dark. Then as each fabric is added to the pile, compare it with the swatch, squinting if necessary. If any mistakes are made, they will show up as soon as a small amount of piecing is begun, and the offending fabric can be moved to the correct pile. It may not be necessary to take apart the one block or small corner that has been pieced, as some variation is often desirable in a scrap pattern.

Then when the fabric is in light, medium, and dark piles, just choose from the correct pile when rotary cutting a fabric for the quilt pattern. Some of the patterns give directions for cutting all the shapes needed. It is best, however, to first cut a small quantity of the colors and shapes required and begin piecing, in case a fabric needs to be moved into a different value pile.

Note: If piecing seams divide one value of the 3-D figure, take care with the direction stripes are cut and pieced, or limit use of these fabrics to unseamed units.

Two striped triangles seamed together

Bottom triangle turned, now stripes flow in the same direction, even if they don't line up perfectly

Tools

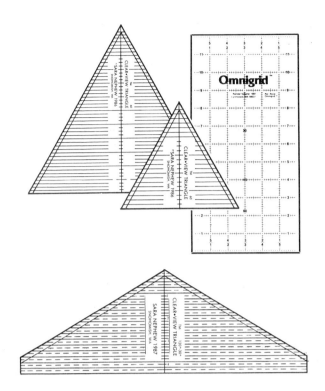

Two key tools go a long way in saving time when making three-sided quilts. The **Clearview Triangle** makes rotary cutting and accurate piecing of 60° triangles, 60° diamonds, hexagons, etc., fast and easy. The Triangles comes in three sizes. The **Clearview Half-Diamond** is designed especially for rotary cutting speed-pieced 60° diamonds divided lengthwise into two different fabrics. It also speeds the cutting of other shapes. These tools are made from $\frac{1}{8}''$ acrylic, for use with a rotary cutter. (See page 64 for ordering information).

Besides Clearview Triangles, required tools are: a rotary cutter, a cutting mat, and a clear, straight ruler like the Salem Rule or Omnigrid (for cutting strips). A large rotary cutter is preferred, since it saves muscle strain, cuts faster, and tends to stay on a straight line. I also like a ruler that measures $6'' \times 12''$ for my strip cutting method (see page 10). The shorter rule is less likely to move during cutting.

Rotary Cutting and Speed Piecing

For a little while, please set aside all thoughts of seam allowances, cardboard templates, and fabric as yardage. Consider only:

1. A strip of fabric;
2. A plastic 60° triangle with a ruled line on the perpendicular.

Every technique in this book is based on these 2 elements. The triangle is laid over the strip in various ways, and a rotary cutter is used along the edges of the triangle to cut off portions of the fabric strip.

Nothing in this book is difficult to do as long as the triangle and the strip are kept in mind. The strip may be changed by making it wider or narrower, or by sewing it to another strip before doing any cutting. The triangle may be changed by making it larger or smaller, or by changing it from a 60° (equilateral) triangle to a 120° half-diamond.

By working just with these elements, **many** shapes can be cut in whatever size desired. These shapes will all fit together to form a design, a quilt top.

After doing a large number of these quilts, I have found that it is not necessary to calculate all measurements each time a new design is cut and pieced. Instead, knowledge of a few basic rules often makes the next step automatic.

The following section first lists the rules and then describes the methods for cutting various shapes, emphasizing the rule for each operation. Please read through the whole section before beginning to piece any of the patterns in this book. The index at the back of the book offers easy access so you can review cutting methods while piecing a particular pattern.

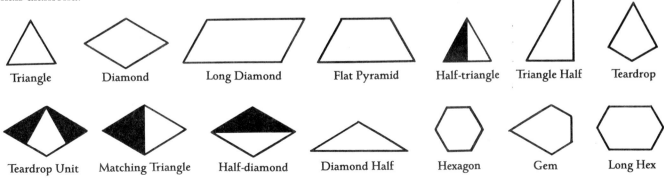

| Triangle | Diamond | Long Diamond | Flat Pyramid | Half-triangle | Triangle Half | Teardrop |

| Teardrop Unit | Matching Triangle | Half-diamond | Diamond Half | Hexagon | Gem | Long Hex |

* Rules

1. Before beginning to cut and piece a design, a **triangle size** is chosen to determine the scale of the design. The triangle size is the perpendicular measurement. A 3″ triangle measures 3″ from tip to base. (A **triangle size** is given for each pattern in the book).

2. A triangle is cut from a strip whose width is the same as the height of the triangle's perpendicular.

3. Diamonds, long diamonds, and flat pyramids are cut from a strip ¼″ narrower than the strip a triangle is cut from.

4. Half-triangles, triangle halves and teardrops are cut from a strip ½″ wider than the strip a triangle is cut from.

5. To draft a hexagon, use a triangle measuring ½″ less than the **triangle size** chosen.

6. A hexagon is cut from a strip whose width is twice the perpendicular of the triangle used to draft the hexagon. (See hexagon table page 14)

* All of the rules and measurements in this book apply if a ¼″ seam is taken.

Cutting Strips

The first step in cutting any shape is cutting strips. All fabric should be prewashed. 100% cotton is preferred.

1. Fold fabric selvage to selvage and press. If pressing from the selvage to the fold produces wrinkles, move the top layer of fabric left or right keeping selvages parallel, until wrinkles disappear.

2. Bring fold to selvage (folding again) and press.

3. Use the wide ruler as a right angle guide, or line up the selvages with the edge of the mat, and the ruler with the mat edge perpendicular to the selvage. Cut off the ragged or irregular edges of the fabric.

4. Cut the strip width required, using the newly cut fabric edge as a guide.

5. Open the strip. It should be straight, not zig zag, if you had the ruler at right angles to the selvages and folds. Adjust the ruler slightly if necessary and trim fabric edges slightly before cutting the next strip.

Cutting Directions

The cutting directions given in this book are essentially the same as those in the previous book, STARS AND FLOWERS: THREE-SIDED PATCHWORK. A few changes and improvements have been made. Also, some of the shapes that can be cut are not needed in these patterns; but I have left the cutting directions in here for those who may devise a 3-D design requiring these shapes.

To cut triangles:

Rule: A triangle is cut from a strip whose width is the same as the height of the triangles' perpendicular. Example: A 3″ triangle is cut from a strip 3″ wide.

1. Position the tip of the Clearview Triangle at one edge of the strip, and the 3″ ruled line at the other edge of the strip.

2. Rotary cut along the 2 sides of the triangle. Move the Clearview Triangle along the same edge (do not flip it to the other side of the fabric strip) for the next cut, lining up the cut point of the fabric strip with the 3″ line on the plastic triangle. Check to be sure the strip edge is right along the ruled line.

3. Cut along both sides of the triangle. (Strips may be stacked up to 8 thicknesses and all cut at once.)

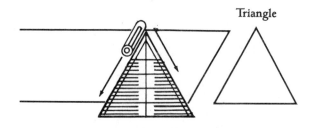

Triangle

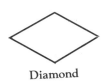

Diamond

1.

2.

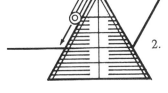

Long Diamond

Flat Pyramid

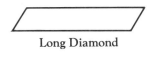

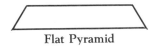

To cut diamonds:

Rule: Diamonds, long diamonds and flat pyramids are cut from a strip ¼″ narrower than the strip a triangle is cut from.

1. Position the Clearview Triangle with one side along one edge of the strip. Strip should be ¼″ narrower than the triangle size chosen for the design. Cut the end of the strip to a 60° angle.

2. Reposition the Clearview Triangle so the tip is at one edge of the strip and a ruled line is along the other edge. (The same position as is used to cut triangles, except the strip is ¼″ narrower.)

3. Rotary cut **only** along the side opposite the first cut.

4. Keep moving the tool along the same side of the strip, lining up the cut edge and the side of the tool as shown. Always cut the side opposite the first cut. (Strips may be stacked up to 8 thicknesses and all cut at once.)

To cut long diamonds and flat pyramids:

Rule: Diamonds, long diamonds and flat pyramids are cut from a strip ¼″ narrower than the strip a triangle is cut from.

Method #1

Trim one end of the strip to a 60° angle. Sew long side of the strip to the piece desired. Trim the other end to the correct angle.

Method #2 (Long Diamond)

1. Trim one end of the strip to a 60° angle.

2. Place the Clearview Triangle over the fabric strip, with a 60° fabric triangle extending from under the tool, and the cut edge lined up at the tool edge. Set the bottom edge of the strip at the measurement given in the pattern, or according to the TABLE OF COMMON SHAPES (pg. 18). Cut the side opposite the first cut.

Method #3 (Flat Pyramid)

Place the Clearview Triangle over the fabric strip, lining up one edge of the strip at the measurement given in the pattern, or according to the TABLE OF COMMON SHAPES (pg. 18). Cut each side of the strip.

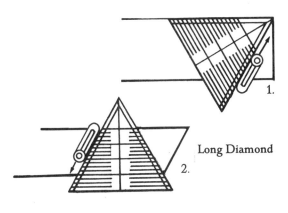

1.

Long Diamond

2.

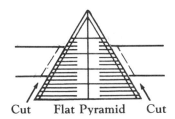

Cut   Flat Pyramid   Cut

Note: care must be taken when cutting long diamonds, as they do have a reverse of their shape. Check carefully to be sure you are cutting them in the direction required by the pattern. If you don't need both the long diamond and its reverse, keep fabric right sides up. Try cutting just one first, to be sure it's right.

To cut a triangle half:

Rule: Half-triangles, triangle halves, and teardrops are cut from a strip ½″ wider than the strip a triangle is cut from.

Method #1

1. Cut triangles from a strip ½″ wider than the triangle size chosen for the design.
2. Bisect these triangles on the perpendicular. Line up the side of the fabric triangle with the perpendicular line of the Clearview Triangle, then cut the fabric triangle in half along the ruler edge.

Method #2

1. Cut a rectangle the height needed for the triangle half and half the width of that triangle's base (measure with a ruler). Then bisect this rectangle from corner to corner diagonally. (This will produce 2 halves the same, rather than a left and a right. Lay the ruler from corner to corner to check and see if this is the shape needed. If not, lay it along the other 2 corners.)

To cut diamond half:

Method #1

Use the Clearview Half-Diamond to rotary cut 120° triangles from the proper width strip. (See the table of measurements for half diamonds on page 16.)

Method #2

1. Line up center line of tool with edge of fabric strip cut at the width required. (See the table of measurements for half diamonds on page 16.)

2. Flip tool, line up center line with strip edge and previous cut at edge of tool. Cut other 30° angle.

Finding the Strip Width for a Half-Diamond or diamond half

(See the table of measurements for half diamonds on page 16.)

Use a fine-tipped pen or sharp pencil and slant it toward the ruler.

1. Using the plastic template, draw your triangle

2. Mark and draw the perpendicular line, extending it below your triangle's perpendicular.

3. Reverse the plastic template. Line it up along the extended perpendicular line, with the base line of the drawn triangle exactly under the same lines less ½″on the plastic template (3½″ for a 4″ triangle.)

4. Draw one side.

5. Add ¼″ seam allowance to the perpendicular line, extending sides to meet.

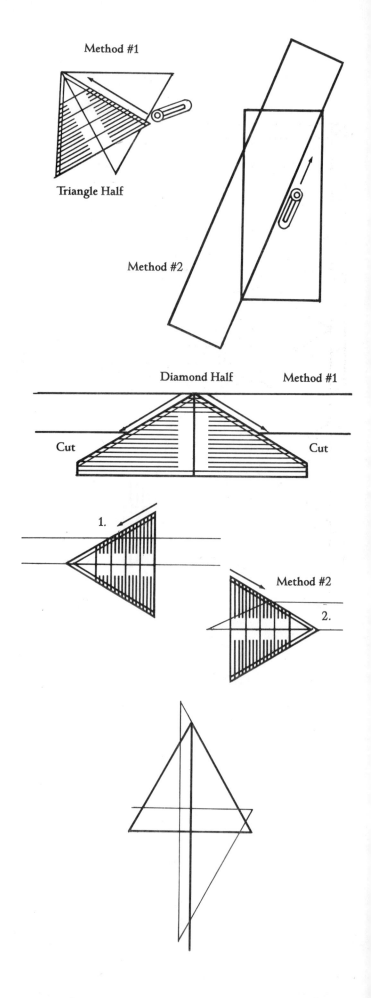

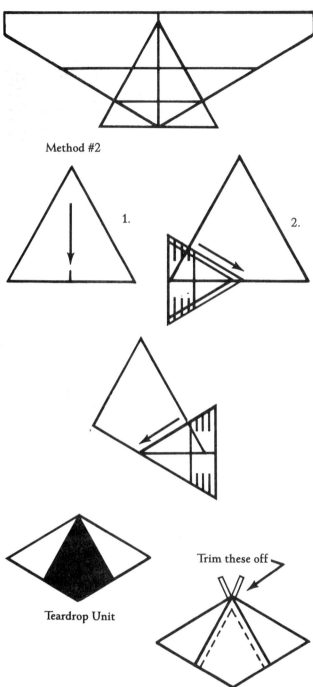

Cut Teardrop Method #1

Method #2

1.

2.

Teardrop Unit

Trim these off

To cut a teardrop:

Rule: Half-triangles, triangle halves, and teardrops are cut from strips ½″ wider than the strip a triangle is cut from.

Method #1

1. Cut triangles from a strip ½″ wider than the **triangle size** required.

2. Position Clearview Half-Diamond on triangle so its tip is opposite triangle tip. Line up the triangle point with the perpendicular of the Half-Diamond and line the triangle sides up evenly with one of the rulings, as shown. Then use rotary cutter to cut the base of the teardrop.

Method #2

1. Cut triangles as #1 above.

2. Measure the base of these triangles and find the center or half measurement.

3. Lay the perpendicular of the Clearview Triangle along the base of the fabric triangle, with the point at center. Rotary cut this wedge off. Reverse the template and cut off the other base corner.

Teardrop Unit

A teardrop unit, made from 1 teardrop shape and 2 triangle halves, is very useful. Seam one triangle half on each side of the teardrop to make a diamond-shaped unit. I line these pieces up for seaming at the bottom, not the top. Press each seam. Trim off the little seam ears to finish. This piece requires careful attention, both in cutting and seaming. If too small, narrower seam width is the solution.

Drafting Hexagons With the Clearview Triangle

To draft an accurate hexagon using the Clearview Triangle, two methods can be used. For method one:

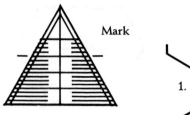

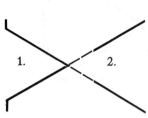

1. Draw two sides of the triangle, marking the desired base line.

2. Extend these lines with a ruler.

3. Position the template along one line and draw the third intersecting line. Extend this line also.

4. Use a compass to draw a circle the marked distance along the lines. (Set the point in the center of the intersecting lines.)

5. Connect the lines at the compass markings.

Method two eliminates the compass. Simply mark the triangle base along each line and connect the marks. Either way, these hexagons include seam allowance.

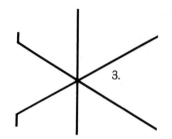

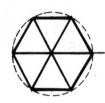

To cut a hexagon:

(It is usually not necessary to actually draft the hexagon.)

Two rules apply

Rule: To draft a hexagon, use a triangle measuring ½″ less than the **triangle size** chosen.

Rule: A hexagon is cut from a strip whose width is twice the perpendicular of the triangle used to draft the hexagon.

SEE TABLE BELOW

Example: **3″ triangle size**—draft the hexagon from 2½″ triangles.

2½″+2½″=5″ strip. This will yield a hexagon that a 3″ triangle will sew on to.

1. Cut a fabric strip according to the pattern directions, or according to the hexagon table below.

2. Cut 60° diamonds from the strip. (See "to cut diamonds", pg. 11).

3. From each end of the diamonds, cut a triangle whose size is ½ of the strip width. Example: 5″ strip means a 2½″ triangle must be removed from each end of each diamond.

Hexagon

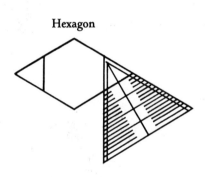

HEXAGON TABLE

Triangle size	Drafting triangle
1″	½″
2″	1½″
3″	2½″
4″	3½″
5″	4½″
6″	5½″

Strip to cut	Cut off triangle
1″	½″
3″	1½″
5″	2½″
7″	3½″
9″	4½″
11″	5½″

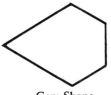

Gem Shape

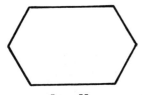

Long Hex

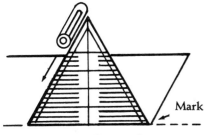

Mark

Cut Long Diamond

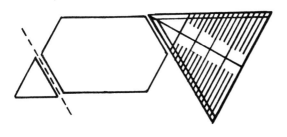

To cut a gem shape

Instead of cutting a hexagon from the diamond, cut only one point off, leaving this shape.

To cut a long hex

1. Cut a strip width according to the HEXAGON TABLE.

2. Cut a long diamond (see pg. 11). The length of the long side is:

Triangle Size	Side Length
2″	4¼″
3″	7¼″
4″	10¼″
5″	13¼″
6″	16¼″

Cut one side, make a pencil mark at the other side, and cut to a 60° angle at this pencil mark.

3. From each end of the long diamond, cut a triangle whose size is ½ of the strip width. (Same as **cutting a hexagon,** page 14.)

(The long hex is not used in any of the patterns given in this book, but could be used in many designs. Example shown.)

Piecing Hints

All my piecing is done with ¼″ seams. Even if the presser foot on your sewing machine features this ¼″ for you, it is a good idea to measure the seams occasionally until you are confident of accuracy. Check to be sure the seam is **just inside** the ¼″ line rather than right on it.

When many seams intersect at one point such as in the Winchester Cathedral quilt, pinch the center where the seams cross, open the fabric to see how the seams are meeting and adjust as necessary. Pin to hold the fabric for seaming.

A few tips about trimming seams are included in the cutting instructions. I trim in a number of places to reduce bulk as the quilt top is pieced. Be careful not to trim too much off before the next step, however, as the little points that stick out help align the parts for accurate sewing. Experience helps. The mild bias of the triangles also aids in lining up seams. Pull a little if necessary. All seams are pressed to one side to make quilting easier.

Sandwich Piecing

To sandwich piece matching triangle units
(sandwich piecing uses 2 strips of fabric):
1. Cut strips of fabric the width of the triangle size. Two different fabrics are used, usually one light and one dark. Seam these strips right sides together with a ¼″ seam down both the right and the left side of the pair of strips. Position the Clearview Triangle so the tip is at one edge of the strips, and the ruled line for the correct size triangle at the other edge. Rotary cut on both sides of the tool. (Same as cutting triangles.)
2. Pull the tips of the seamed triangles apart and press open.

To sandwich piece half-diamond units
1. Cut strips of fabric whose width equals the perpendicular measurement of one-half the unit desired, including seam allowance, or according to the measurements given in the half-diamond table below. Two different fabrics are used, usually one light and one dark.
2. Sew light and dark strips right sides together with a ¼″ seam allowance down each side.
3. Using a Clearview Half-Diamond and a rotary cutter, cut triangles from the seamed strips. Line up the ruler tip at one seamed edge, and the desired line on the ruler at the other edge, and cut as for triangles.
4. Use a seam ripper to cut one stitch at the seamed tip of the fabric 120° triangles.
5. Pull the tips of the seamed triangles apart and press open, pressing across the width of the diamond and pulling the top and bottom out straight while pressing.
6. Trim off the little seam ears as shown.

HALF-DIAMOND TABLE

Triangle Size	Strip Width
2″	1¼″
3″	1⅞″
4″	2⅜″

Triangle Size	Strip Width
5″	3″
6″	3½″

To sandwich piece half-triangle units:
Rule: Half-triangles, triangle halves, and teardrops are cut from a strip ½″ wider than the strip a triangle is cut from.
1. Cut two fabric strips ½″ wider than the **triangle size.** Usually a dark and a light are used. Press these right sides together.

2. On the Clearview Triangle, measure ½ the base of the triangle with the perpendicular measurement of the two fabric strips, OR USE HALF-TRIANGLE TABLE BELOW.
3. On the light colored fabric, draw lines as far apart as ½ the base of this triangle. Pencil, chalk or washout blue lines are all fine.
4. Seam through both strips ¼″ away on both sides of all the lines drawn. Press flat again.
5. Cut triangles from the strips, lining up the perpendicular of the ruler with the drawn line, and cutting as for triangles.
6. Bisect each triangle on the drawn line, using a rotary cutter or scissors. Pull tips apart and press open. This yields right and left half-triangle units.

HALF-TRIANGLE TABLE

Triangle Size	Strip Width	Distance Between Lines
2″	2½″	1½″
3″	3½″	2⅛″
4″	4½″	2⅝″
5″	5½″	3¼″
6″	6½″	3¹³⁄₁₆″

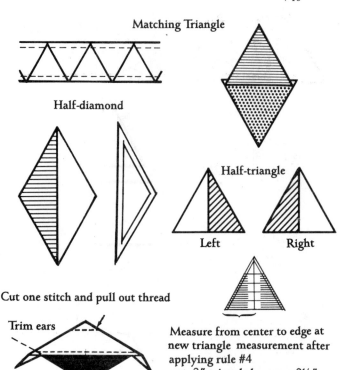

Matching Triangle

Half-diamond

Half-triangle

Left　　Right

Cut one stitch and pull out thread

Trim ears

Measure from center to edge at new triangle measurement after applying rule #4
ext. 3″ triangle becomes 3½″

Seam Lines　　Pencil Line

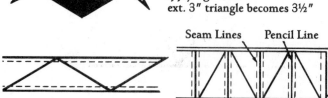

Enlarging or Shrinking a Pattern

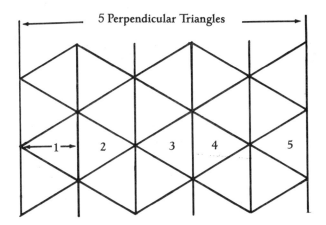

5 Perpendicular Triangles

1   2   3   4   5

3″ Design Triangle

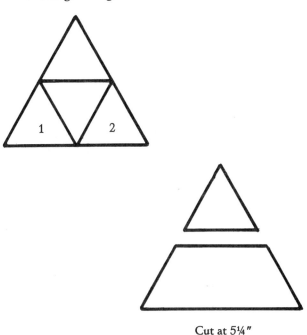

Cut at 5¼″

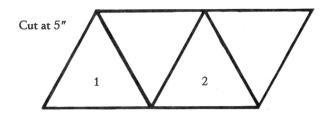

Cut at 5″

It's fun to try substituting a different **triangle size** when piecing a particular quilt design. Following are instructions on how to do a rough estimate of how altering triangle size will change the size of the quilt. (To calculate new dimensions exactly, see pg. 19).

The perpendicular triangle measurement is easy to figure. Just subtract ¾″ from the triangle size chosen to obtain "finished" height and multiply by the number of triangles perpendicular across the grid of the quilt design. (If this is not easily seen, sketch the design on graph paper.)

By comparing the new measurement with the original, you can then estimate the other dimension of the quilt. Let's use 3 BLOCKS–VARIATION (pg. 22).

The body of the quilt, without borders, has 12 perpendicular triangles across the width. Using a 3″ triangle size, the quilt width is 27″ (2¼″×12) without borders. Changing to a 2″ triangle size results in a width of 15″ (1¼″×12) without borders, almost ½ the width of the larger quilt. Half the width and ½ the length would mean a quilt about ¼ the size. In this quilt, the change would be from a baby quilt to a doll quilt by reducing one triangle size.

To substitute a new triangle size follow the RULES and CUTTING DIRECTIONS for all the standard pieces. For larger pieces, or for flat pyramids, etc. the following information and table will be helpful. Use this information to change the size of shapes or to find the size of a shape in an original design.

When a shape is on graph paper, it can be analyzed and its size determined using simple math. Count the rows in the shape.

Example: This shape is composed of a triangle and a flat pyramid. Triangle cut from 3″ strip, loses ¼″ seam when sewed to flat pyramid. Flat pyramid cut from 2¾″ strip, loses ¼″ seam when sewed to triangle.

Result: 2¾″ triangle height + 2½″ flat pyramid height so shape is cut at 5¼″ line on Clearview Triangle. (All the math in this example is based on a 3″ triangle size).

The long diamond is a special case. It uses the same measurement as the other shapes, minus ¼″.

EX. Table of common shapes shows 2 triangles on base of shape. 3″ triangle size-cut at 5¼″ on the Clearview Triangle. A long diamond is needed with 2 triangles on the bottom side. Cut at 5″ on the Clearview Triangle–¼″ less than the table measurement for the triangle or flat pyramid.

Common Shapes

Design Triangle size	Use this base line on the Clearview Triangle
2″	3¼″
3″	5¼″
4″	7¼″
5″	9¼″
6″	11¼″

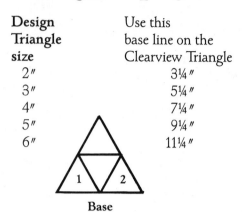

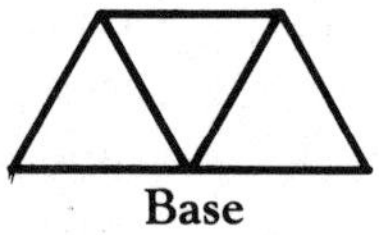

Base

Design Triangle size	Use this base line on the Clearview Triangle
2″	4½″
3″	7½″
4″	10½″
5″	13½″
6″	16½″

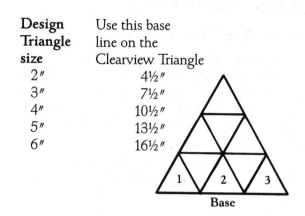

Base

Design Triangle size	Use this base line on the Clearview Triangle
2″	5¾″
3″	9¾″
4″	13¾″
5″	17¾″
6″	21¾″

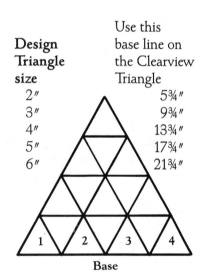

Base

Flat Pyramid

Design Triangle size

2″	3¼″	Use this base line on the Clearview Triangle
3″	5¼″	
4″	7¼″	
5″	9¼″	
6″	11¼″	

Base

Flat Pyramid

Design Triangle size	Use this base line on the Clearview Triangle
2″	4½″
3″	7½″
4″	10½″
5″	13½″
6″	16½″

Base

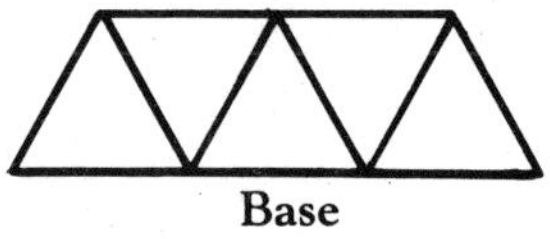

Long Diamond

Design Triangle size	Use this base line on the Clearview Triangle
2″	3″
3″	5″
4″	7″
5″	9″
6″	11″

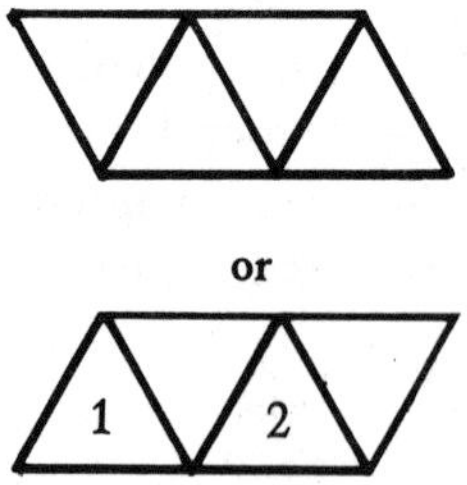

or

Example: To change a 2″ triangle pattern to a 3″ pattern, follow the tables above and when the dimension called for is 3¼″, subsitute 5¼″; when the dimension called for is 5¾″, substitute 9¾″; etc.

The Quilts

How to Use These Diagrams

These quilt diagrams depict each design by value, showing only light, medium, dark, and background shades. Substitute your own fabric in these values, whether plaid, flowered, or plain-colored. Value (lightness or darkness of shading) is the most important consideration.

To follow the cutting directions given for each quilt or block, please note: often cutting directions are given completely, including:

1. strip width, and
2. line used on Clearview Triangle.

If these are not both included, then a rule applies. The rules are listed on pg. 10 and with each cutting method described. (See index pg. 63 to find page numbers for all cutting directions.)

For example: if directions say, "Cut a flat pyramid from a 2¾″ strip at 9¾″," strip width is given, and the line on the triangle is given. (The person cutting, if unfamiliar with the methods, may still need to review pg. 11 to see how to cut a flat pyramid.)

The next direction may say: "Cut a flat pyramid at 7½″." Strip width is not given, so a rule applies. The rule is applied using the triangle size given for the whole design at the very beginning of each pattern, and is the basic measurement for all cutting and piecing techniques in that pattern. Familiarity will make the methods very easy.

Fabic requirements given for each pattern are for 45″ wide pre-washed cotton or cotton blends.

Determining Size of a Finished Quilt

To calculate the size of a finished quilt, two triangle measurements are needed: the perpendicular of the triangle without seam allowance (always ¾″ less than **triangle size**), and the length of the triangle **side** without seam allowances, which can be measured with a ruler on the Clearview Triangle. (Or use the table below.)

Multiply the "finished" perpendicular height by the number of triangles in one perpendicular line across the quilt. Multiply the "finished" triangle side by the number of sides across the other quilt dimension.

These two calculations will give you the measurements of the finished size of the quilt.

Table of Finished Triangles
(when using ¼″ seams)

Triangle Size	Finished Perpendicular	Finished Side Length
1″	¼″	$5/16$″
2″	1¼″	$1 7/16$″
3″	2¼″	$2 5/8$″
4″	3¼″	$3 13/16$″
5″	4¼″	$4 15/16$″
6″	5¼″	$6 1/8$″
7″	6¼″	$7 1/4$″
8″	7¼″	$8 7/16$″
9″	8¼″	$9 9/16$″
10″	9¼″	$10 3/4$″
11″	10¼″	$11 7/8$″
12″	11¼″	$13 1/16$″

Note: The diagrams usually consist of combinations of the symbols for individual units (ex. half-diamond ◆ *) showing proper placement in sections, rows, etc., rather than a sketch of how the seaming actually looks when incomplete. So 2 half-diamonds sewn together would be shown as number 1 rather than number 2 (which is closer to the way they might actually look). Also when individual instructions are not given for a triangle's size, it is the same as the triangle size given at the beginning of the pattern.*

Number 1   **Number 2**

Box of Tricks

3″ triangle

To piece one unit cut:

2 background 3″ triangles
2 medium 3″ triangles
1 dark diamond
1 light diamond

Assemble into 2 sections as shown and seam into one diamond-shaped unit. Make larger blocks from 4 units as shown. Make as many blocks as needed for the size of quilt desired. (See tables below.) Seam blocks into rows. Finish ends of rows with a 10¼″ background triangle half from a 10¼″×6″ rectangle bisected diagonally as shown. Sew the rows together. Add a 2¼″ border of background fabric at left and right sides. Then add a 4″ outer border of plain fabric.

Note: Arrows show direction to sew on medium triangles when dealing with a stripe or plaid.

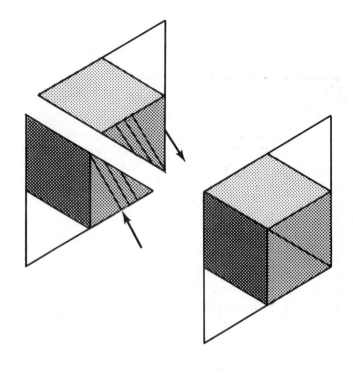

Piecing Diagram   One Unit

Quilt size with borders
38″×50¼″–Baby
3 rows wide
each row 3 blocks
cut pieces for
1 unit × 36
Fabric requirements:
½ yd. each of light,
medium, dark, and
⅞ yd. background fabrics
¾ yd. border fabric

Quilt size with borders
47″×58¼″–Youth
4 rows wide
each row 4 blocks
cut pieces for
1 unit × 64
Fabric requirements:
⅔ yd. each of light,
medium, dark, and
1 yd. background fabrics
¾ yd. border fabric

Quilt size with borders
56″×68¾″–Throw
5 rows wide
each row 5 blocks
cut pieces for 1 unit
× 100
Fabric requirements:
1 yd. each of light,
medium, dark, and
1⅓ yds. background
fabrics
1 yd. border fabric

Quilt size with borders
65″×79¼″–Twin
6 rows wide
each row 6 blocks
cut pieces for
1 unit × 144
Fabric requirements:
1½ yds. each of
light, medium, dark and
2 yds. background fabrics
1¼ yds. border fabric

Quilt size with borders
83″×100¼″–Double
8 rows wide
each row 8 blocks
cut pieces for
1 unit × 225
Fabric requirements:
2¼ yds. each of
light, medium, dark and
3 yds. background fabrics
1½ yds. border fabric

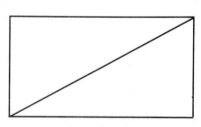

Bisect rectangle

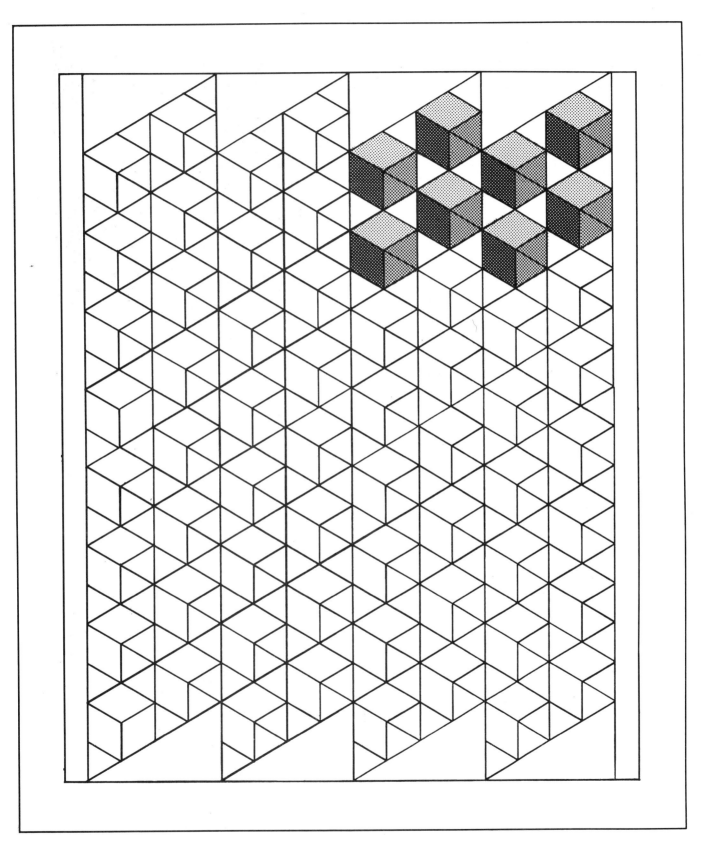

3 Blocks-Variation

3" triangle

Quilt with borders:
36"×42"

Fabric requirements:

⅔ yd. dark fabric
⅔ yd. medium fabric
⅔ yd. light fabric
1½ yds. background fabric
½ yd. dark border fabric

Directions:

1. Cut for one block:
   2 background 5¼" triangles
   2 light diamonds cut from 2¾" strip
   2 medium diamonds
   2 dark diamonds
   2 light 3" triangles
   2 medium 3" triangles
   2 dark 3" triangles
   6 background 3" triangles

2. Piece in wedges as shown. Add 5¼" background triangles to make the complete diamond-shaped block. Make 3 more of these. Piece 4 corner blocks, using 2 triangle halves cut from a 5¾" triangle at the top or bottom of the block as shown.

3. Use 2 blocks to make row B. Cut 2 background pieces 9½"×9½". Trim both to 60° angle (see quilt diagram). Use to finish Row B.

4. Use 2 blocks and 4 corner blocks to make 2 of row A. Seam rows A and B together alternately, according to the quilt diagram. To make a larger quilt, just make more blocks and more rows.

5. Add a 2¾" inner border of background fabric. Laurie added a 2½" dark outer border and plaid bias binding to complete the quilt.

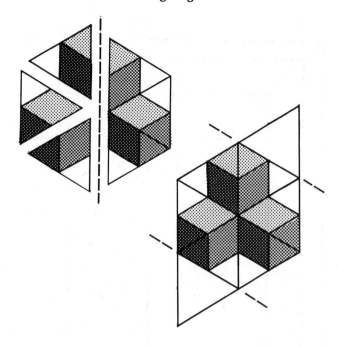

Piecing Diagram

Partial blocks

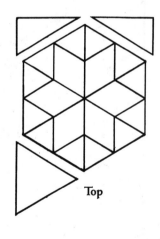

Top

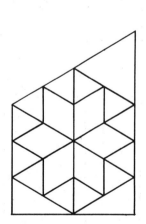

Bottom

3 Blocks-Variation

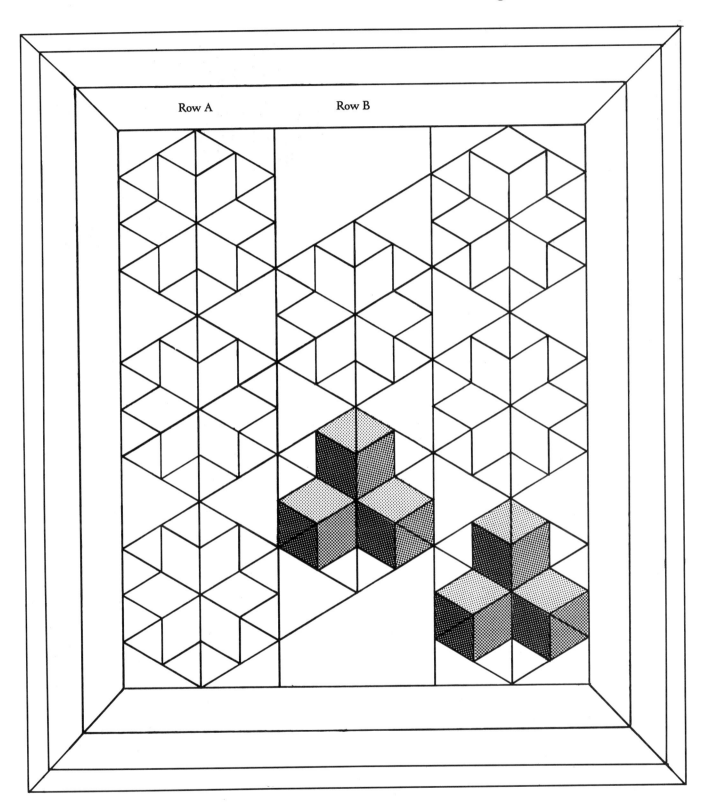

Row A   Row B

Tumbling Blocks

3″ triangle

Quilt with borders: 35½″×42½″

Fabric requirements:

⅔ yd. dark fabric
⅔ yd. medium fabric
⅔ yd. light fabric
⅓ yd. background fabric
⅔ yd. border fabric
(If using more than one
fabric in a value group, buy
at least a 6″ width of each
fabric to allow for shrinkage,
off-grain weaves, etc.)

Directions:

1. Cut for each half-block:
1 dark diamond (from 2¾″ strip)
1 medium diamond
1 light diamond
1 dark 3″ triangle
1 medium triangle
1 light triangle

2. Make 21 half-blocks as shown. Sew 18 of these into complete blocks. Make 3 rows of 3 blocks each.

3. Using a half-block, a dark triangle, a medium diamond, a light triangle half from a 3½″ triangle, (left side, the right side will be used in #4 below) and a light diamond half from a 1⅞″ strip, assemble 1 partial block. Make 2 more of these.

4. Using a dark diamond, a medium triangle, a light triangle half (right side) and a light diamond half, assemble 1 fill-in piece. Make 2 more of these.

5. Add a fill-in piece alternately to the top or bottom of each row, and a partial block to the other end of each row as shown in quilt diagram. Seam the three rows together.

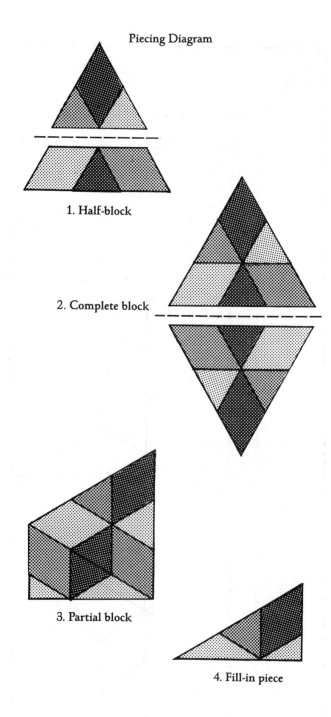

Piecing Diagram

1. Half-block

2. Complete block

3. Partial block

4. Fill-in piece

Optional:

6. Piece a left and right border to complete the blocks. The left border is assembled from medium diamonds, light triangles, and background flat pyramids cut from a 2¾″ strip at 5¼″ on the Clearview Triangle. The right border uses dark rather than medium diamonds. Cut one background diamond and use it at the upper right. Finish borders top and bottom with a light 3½″ triangle half. Add additional borders as desired. I used a 1¾″ strip of black and a 4″ strip of large print.

Tumbling Blocks

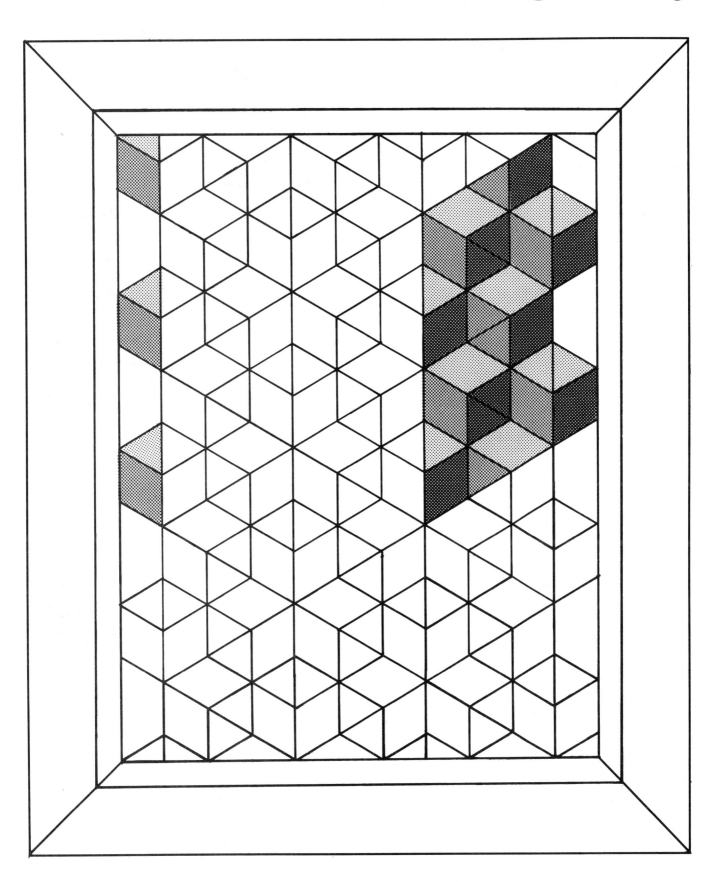

Tumbling Through Space

Tumbling Through Space

4″ triangle

Quilt without borders:
58½″×91½″

Fabric requirements:

1¼ yd. dark fabric
1½ yd. medium fabric
1¼ yd. light fabric
2½ yds. background fabric
1½ yds. border fabric

Directions for each block:

Bricks and Blocks Turned

1. Cut:
2 light long diamonds (one and its reverse) at 7″ on
Clearview Triangle from 3¾″ strip.
2 medium long diamonds at 7″
2 dark long diamonds at 7″
2 light diamonds from 3¾″ strip
2 medium diamonds
2 dark diamonds
4 light 4″ triangles
4 medium 4″ triangles
4 dark 4″ triangles
6 background 4″ triangles

2. Piece in wedges as shown.
Each wedge contains this unit (a diamond and 2
triangles) and this unit or its reverse (a long diamond and
a triangle). Color values must be placed according to the
diagram. Make 2 more of these.
Add on either side of each block a 10½″ background
triangle as shown.

Bricks and Blocks

1. Cut: same as above.

2. Place in wedges as shown (not as above). Make one
more of these.

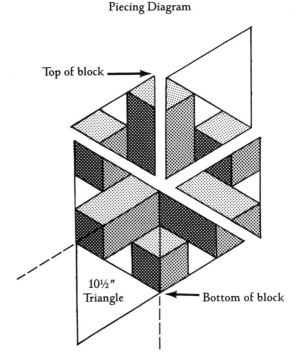

Piecing Diagram

Bricks and Blocks Turned

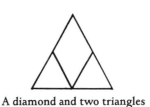

A diamond and two triangles

A long diamond and a triangle

One Block Variation

1. Cut:
7 light diamonds from 3¾" strip
7 dark diamonds
14 medium 4" triangles
12 background 4" triangles

2. Piece the center triangle using one pieced cube and 3 background triangles.

3. Add 2 pieced cubes along one side, using 2 background triangles.

4. Add 2 cubes along another side, with 3 background triangles.

5. Add 2 cubes on the last side, with 4 background triangles, to complete the hexagonal block. Make 2 more of these. Add on either side of each block a 10½" background triangle as shown.

Tumbling Blocks and Stars

1. Cut:
1 background 10½" triangle
6 light diamonds
6 dark diamonds
12 medium 4" triangles
9 background 4" triangles

2. Assemble around center triangle as in **One Block Variation.** Add on either side of each block a 10½" background triangle as shown.

3. Make 4 more of these blocks using two 11" background triangle halves on one end of each. These are corner blocks.

4. Assemble 2 partial blocks as shown, using for each partial block:
1 background 10½" triangle
1 background 11" triangle half
3 background 4" triangles
3 light diamonds
3 dark diamonds
6 medium 4" triangles
3 background 4½" triangle halves

5. Assemble quilt in rows as shown, using corner blocks at top and bottom of the outside rows, and partial blocks at top and bottom of the center row. Add borders as desired.

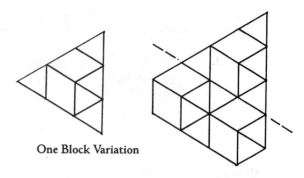

One Block Variation

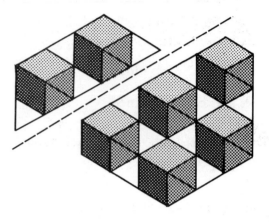

Tumbling Blocks and Stars

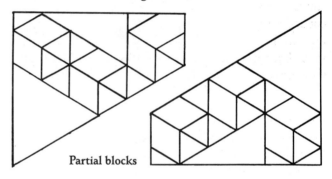

Partial blocks

Bottom corner block

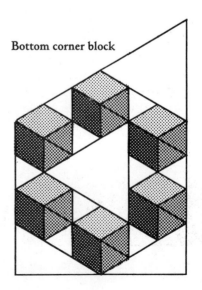

Paintbox, 21½″ × 24½″, is a small color wheel as well as a 3-D project showing various views of a hollow pieced box. Use scraps and a little time to make this wall hanging for your studio/sewing room. Designed, pieced, and machine quilted by Charisa Martin Anderson. (Left)

Babylon, 65″×76¼″. The title of this quilt was inspired by its floral prints and bright pastels, combined with the strong architectural geometry of the pattern. The author was reminded of the biblical "hanging gardens of Babylon." A wide plain border with elaborate quilting helps hold it all together. Quilted by Shirley Gylleck. (Right)

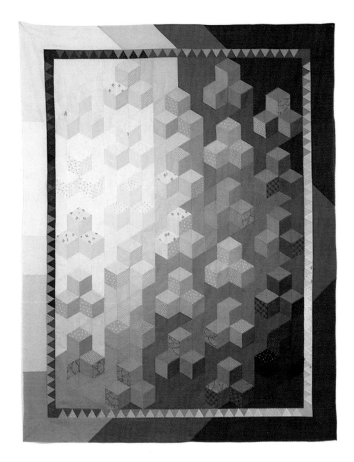

3 Blocks, 56½″ × 73″. Both the background and foreground of this quilt have been shaded from the left, light to dark. The cut fabric shapes were put up on a quilt wall. When the desired effect was achieved the blocks were constructed. The quilt pattern is very simple, however, and blocks could easily be made and basic 3–D effects achieved without this level of planning. Pieced by Laura Munson Reinstatler. (Right)

Winchester Cathedral, 65½″ × 76½″, uses two variations of the same block to produce girders and carved stone flowers. Look through the screen to see stars and a sky dirtied with clouds. Quilted by Maurine Eggertsen. (Left)

Study: Child's Play, 58½″ × 72¼″. This interesting piece is a sampler of 3–D quilt blocks. Many more blocks are possible, but this design was complete. The range of soft shades in the hand–dyed fabric adds a gentle radiance to the quilt. The author used Baptist Fan as an allover quilting pattern for the background, but quilted each shape to make it more dimensional. (Right page)

Honeycomb Waffle, 60″ × 72¾″, is an example of how a large–print type of fabric works effectively in a 3–D design. Plain fabrics are used in the light and dark colors. In the medium color, a swirly crumple–dyed fabric makes the blocks look as if they are made of marble. The many pastels mix for a gently pleasing effect. Pieced by Joan Hanson. (Right)

Tumbling Blocks, 35½″ × 42½″, is fun to piece. Each individual block as it's sewed doesn't look 3–D. But when the finished blocks are laid out together, suddenly cubes start to pop up all over. Quilted by Rose Herrera. (Left)

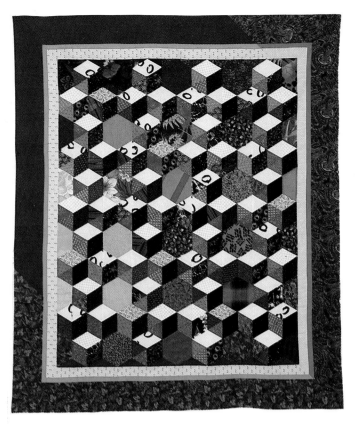

Trellis, 49″ × 57½″, sets off a strong white, grey and black 3–D effect with a crisp undersea background of blue, green and turquoise. This piece has an oriental look, perhaps because some large–scale prints have been used. Pieced by Elizabeth Sevy. (Left)

Emily's Daydream, 42″ × 60″. A castle of hollow boxes with all flags flying...away! No pattern given. Designed by Brad Anderson and Charisa Martin Anderson, pieced and quilted by Laurie Vilbrandt, Elizabeth Sevy, Mary Rathke and Charisa. (Bottom)

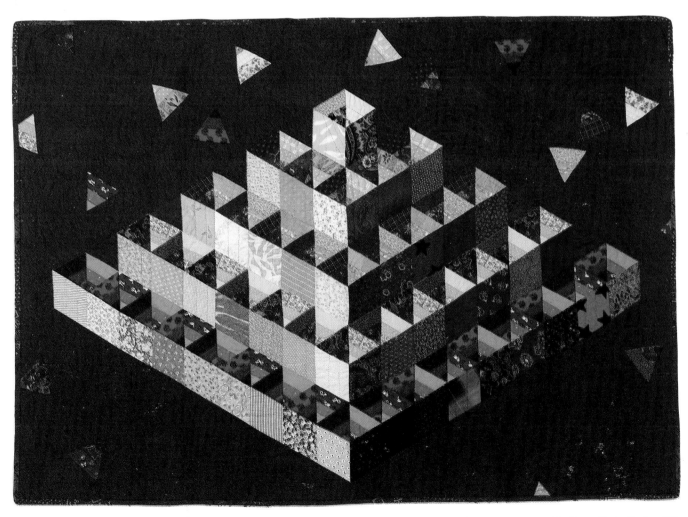

Strip City, *79¾″ × 97¼″.* This quilt includes additional cube borders to finish the edges of the pattern. Scraps of modern fabrics are combined with some pieces from my garage–sale collection. This quilt will look good on a bed or a wall. Quilted by Beverly Payne.

Tumbling Through Space, 58½″ × 91½″, combines three different blocks to build a design like a space station on the day side of the planet with bright stars around it. Each block in this sampler could be used to make a separate quilt design. Pieced and machine quilted by Annette Austin. (Top Left)

Cityscape, 53″ × 66″, shows buildings from many different perspectives. This quilt was assembled in three large sections, at which point a set-in seam was used to finish putting the top together. The background is quilted in gentle curves and in the foreground the angular shapes are emphasized. No pattern given. (Top Right)

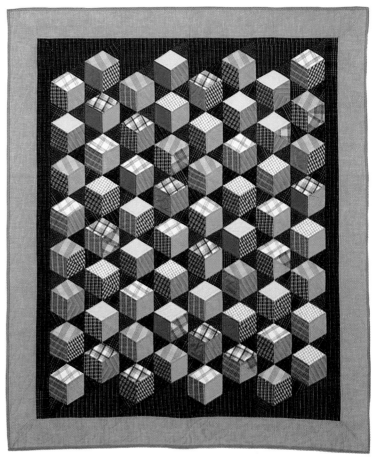

Box of Tricks, 47″ × 58¼″, uses plaids and stripes to emphasize the box shape. Even the background fabric is a plaid. The author chose soft pinks and blues to make this a baby quilt. Quilted by Beverly Payne. (Bottom)

3 Blocks Variation, 36″ × 42″, combines tie silks with a homespun–like plaid to achieve a masculine and very old–fashioned look. The silks add brilliance to the 3–D effect. Pieced by Laurie Vilbrandt. (Top)

The Block Building, 47½″×64″. Seminole piecing is used to light windows in these buildings. Fabric choices were planned by glueing tiny scraps to a piece of tracing paper laid over the black and white quilt diagram. The full size cut shapes were placed on a quilt wall to decide final color placement. Pieced by Laura Munson Reinstatler. (Bottom Left)

Miami Condo, 60½″ × 78″. This building is reminiscent of pastel terraces and sandy beaches. The grey and tan wall on the left side of the building turns the corner, emphasizing the 3–D illusion. Quilted by Maurine Eggertsen. (Bottom Right)

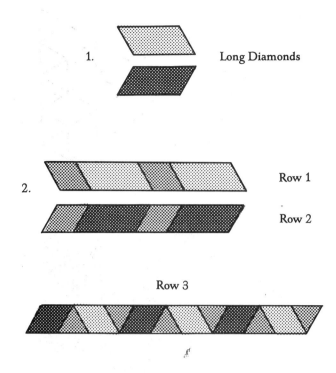

1.   Long Diamonds

2.   Row 1

Row 2

Row 3

Strip City

3″ triangle

Full size quilt with borders
79¾″ × 97¼″

Yardage requirements:

3 yds. assorted dark fabrics
3 yds. assorted medium fabrics
3 yds. assorted light fabrics

Plus: 1¼ yd. dark fabric for inside 3″ plain border
       1½ yd. dark fabric for outside
           4¼″ plain border.

This quilt is pieced using a row method. The smaller quilt in the same pattern on pg. 40 is pieced using a block method.

1. Cutting directions: (Cut long diamonds from 2¾″ strip. Cut as for diamonds at 5″ on the Clearview Triangle.) Note: special attention must be given when cutting the long diamonds. The dark and light pieces are cut at different angles. Strips must be laid out right sides up, and the proper angle cut. Try a few cuts on a single strip first before stacking and cutting large quantities. Cut and piece a small corner of the quilt first, to test the color and value choices.

Cut for body of quilt:
77 light long diamonds at 5″
68 dark long diamonds at 5″
137 medium diamonds
81 dark diamonds
72 light diamonds
161 medium triangles
18 light triangles
7 medium triangle halves
4 dark triangle halves
8 light diamond halves

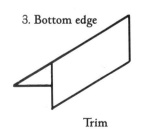

3. Bottom edge

Trim

2. The body of the STRIP CITY quilt is assembled in 3 main sections: a top corner, a bottom corner, and the center. (See diagram). Three rows make up the main pattern. From the top of the center section ...
Row 1 — medium diamond and light long diamond
Row 2 — medium diamond and dark long diamond
Row 3 — medium triangle, light diamond,
           medium triangle, dark diamond

The center section repeats these 3 rows 5 times, with a medium triangle or dark diamond filling the ends of rows 1 and 2 at the left, and a light triangle or medium triangle filling the ends of rows 1 and 3 at the right. (SEE DIAGRAM). Sew these rows together in sets of three, then sew the 5 sets together.

3. The top and bottom corners are assembled from the same rows, but the diagram must be followed to reduce the row length. The rows are begun or ended with diamonds, diamond halves, etc., according to the quilt diagram. (At the bottom, I sewed medium triangle halves to the upper end of the dark long diamonds, and trimmed the excess dark fabric off after the rows were sewn together.)

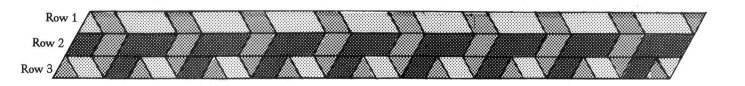

Row 1
Row 2
Row 3

Block Borders

Cut for block borders:
26 light diamonds
28 medium diamonds
55 dark diamonds
59 light triangles
1 dark triangle
26 light diamond halves
26 dark diamond halves
9 dark flat pyramids cut at 5¼ "
    on the Clearview Triangle
9 medium flat pyramids cut at 5¼ "
2 light triangle halves
2 dark triangle halves

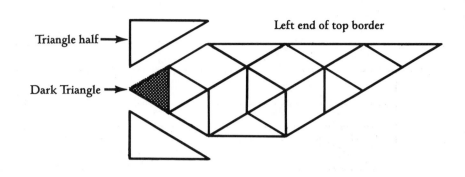

Triangle half →

Left end of top border

Dark Triangle →

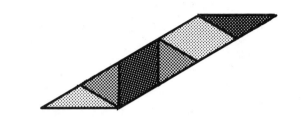

4. Side borders are made from 2 rows. The inner row on each side is a repeat of dark and medium diamonds with light triangles. The outer row on the left repeats black or medium flat pyramids, medium diamonds, and light triangles. The outer row on the right repeats black flat pyramids, dark diamonds, and light triangles. The top and bottom block border is assembled in short diagonal rows as shown.

5. Finish with dark and medium triangle halves cut at 5¼ " on the Clearview Triangle. Place dark at upper left and medium at lower right.

6. Complete the quilt top with a 3 " inner border strip and a 4¼ " outer border, both of dark fabrics.

Diagonal row for
top and bottom border

1 dark diamond half (1⅞" strip)
1 light diamond half (1⅞" strip)
1 dark diamond
1 light diamond
2 medium 3" triangles

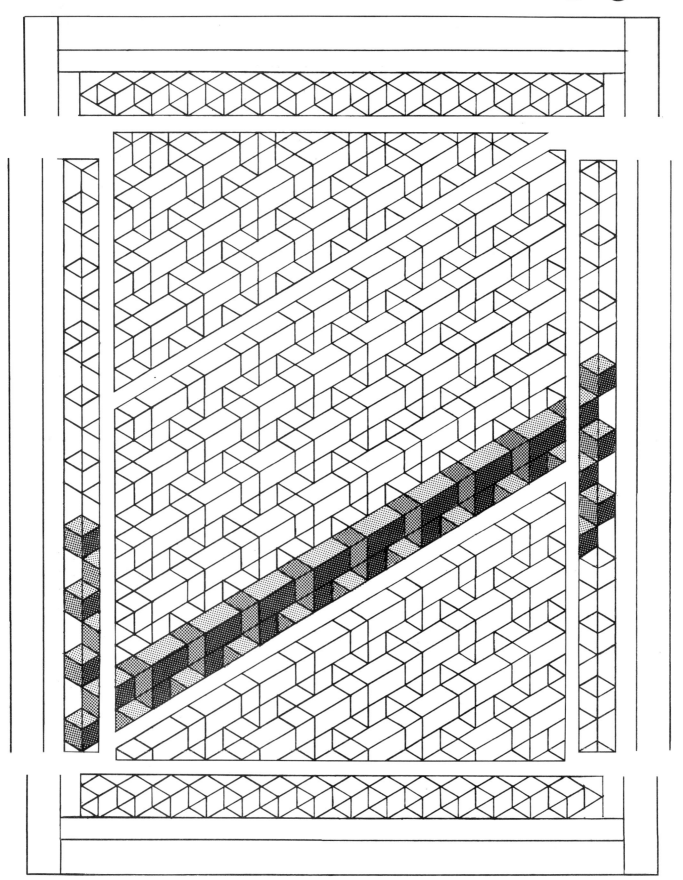

Babylon

3 " triangle

Quilt with borders
65" × 76¼"

Fabric requirements:

Body of quilt:
2½ yds. dark fabric
2½ yds. medium fabric
2½ yds. light fabric
Borders:
1 yd. inner border
2⅛ yds. outer border

Directions:

1. Cut for one block:
2 light flat pyramids from 2¾" strip at 5¼" on the
Clearview Triangle
2 dark flat pyramids
2 medium diamonds from 2¾" strip
2 medium 3" triangles.

2. Assemble into top and bottom sections as shown.
Seam together into block. Make a total of 39 blocks.
Make 3 extra top sections and 3 extra bottom sections.

3. Make 3 rows of 7 blocks. Finish the rows with top
and bottom fill-in pieces. Top fill-in pieces are assembled
from 1 light flat pyramid cut at 5¼", a medium diamond
half from a 1⅞" strip, and a 3½" triangle half. Bottom
fill-in pieces are assembled from dark or medium (see left
or right) flat pyramids and dark or medium 5¾" triangle
halves. After seaming, trim off edge of flat pyramid even
with bottom edge of triangle half.

4. Make 3 rows of 6 blocks, adding a bottom block
section to the top of these rows and a top block section
to the bottom of these rows. Finish with left and right
top and bottom fill-in pieces.

5. Piece 8 left and 8 right border blocks according to
diagrams at right, but use 3½" triangle halves for top
blocks at left and right. (See quilt diagram.) Make left
and right partial blocks at bottom, using the top row of
each border block and adding a 5¾" dark triangle half
to each.

6. Add borders as desired. Shown are a 2" inner border
and a 7" outer border. Sew both strips together,
matching centers. Mark and match centers on the quilt
and on the borders. Sew on from seam allowance to
seam allowance, mitering corners.
(Measurements include seam allowance.)

Piecing Diagram

· 2. Bottom section

Top section

Babylon Block

Top fill-in pieces

Left

Right

Left

Right

(Trim off excess flat pyramid)

Bottom fill-in pieces

Right border block

(med triangle, light 5¼" flat pyramid, dark 5" long
diamond, dark diamond, medium diamond)

Left border block

(dark triangle, light 5¼" flat pyramid, med long
diamond at 5", dark diamond, medium diamond)

Right side of fabric

Honeycomb Waffle

3″ triangle

Quilt with borders:
60″ × 72¾″

Fabric requirements:

2¼ yds. dark fabric (3 or more colors)
2¼·yds. medium fabric (3 or more colors)
2¼ yds. light fabric (3 or more colors)

For borders:

½ yd. light gray
1 yd. dark gray

Directions:

1. For quilt and side borders cut:
64 light flat pyramids cut at 5¼″ on the Clearview
   Triangle
64 dark flat pyramids at 5¼″
64 medium flat pyramids at 5¼″
64 light 3″ triangles
64 mediium 3″ triangles
64 dark 3″ triangles
6 light 5¼″ triangles
3 medium diamonds from 5″ strip
3 dark diamonds from 5″ strip
10 light 5¾″ triangle halves
5 dark 5¾″ triangle halves
5 medium 5¾″ triangle halves

2. Piece 32 each of these 6 wedges.

triangle		flat pyramid	
1. light	–	dark	
2. medium	–	dark	right half-hexagon
3. medium	–	light	
4. light	–	medium	
5. dark	–	medium	left half-hexagon
6. dark	–	light	

   Joan Hanson, who pieced the quilt top shown in color
on pg. 32, adds this pressing hint: when pressing the
wedges, press even-numbered rows (see quilt diagram) to
the narrow point of the wedge and press odd-numbered
rows to the wide base of the wedge. This makes seaming easier and reduces bulk in the completed seams.

3. Assemble into 32 left half-hexes and 32 right
half-hexes.

4. Assemble 28 of each into 8 rows as shown in quilt
diagram with 7 half-hexes to each row. Finish the top of
each row with light triangle halves. Finish the bottom
of each with medium and dark triangle halves
alternately. Sew rows together.

5. Make left and right borders from remaining pieces as
indicated in the quilt diagram.

6. The quilt top is completed with a 2″ light gray inner
border and a 6½″ dark gray outer border. (All
measurements include seam allowance.)

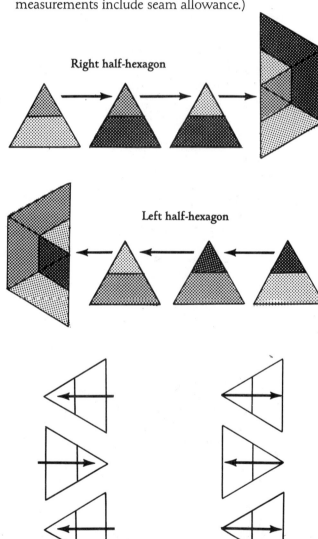

Right half-hexagon

Left half-hexagon

Even—press to point   **Odd—press to base**

*Note: Make this quilt larger or smaller by always increasing
number or length of rows by 2 half-hexagons. (Or change triangle
size.)*

Honeycomb Waffle

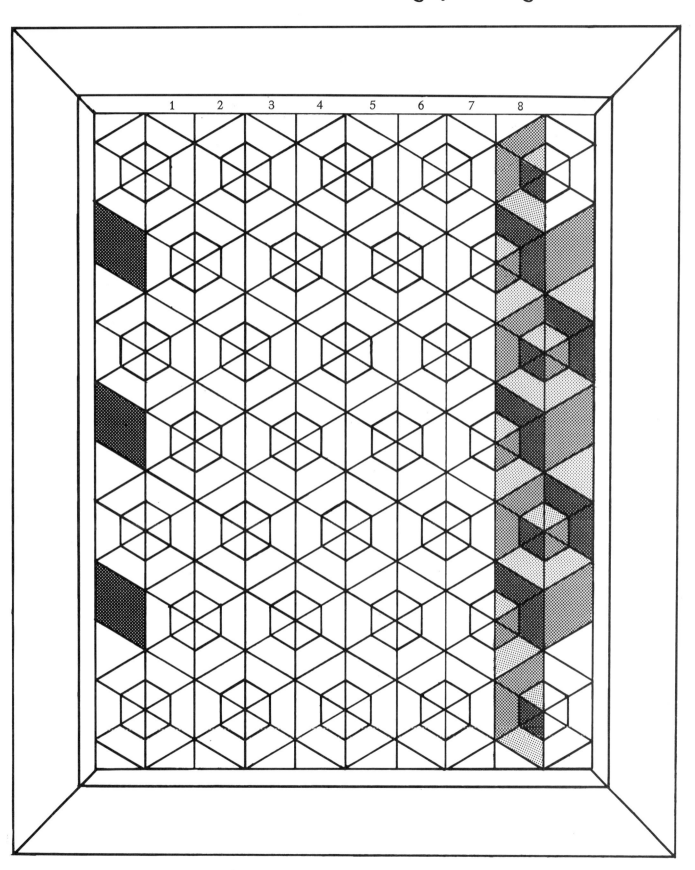

Trellis

3″ triangle

Quilt with borders:
49″ × 57½″

Fabric requirements:

1 yd. assorted dark prints
1¼ yds. assorted medium prints
1½ yds. assorted light prints
1½ yds. background fabric

for borders:

½ yd. light
⅓ yd. medium
1 yd. dark

Directions:

1. Cut for whole quilt:
   64 dark diamonds
   5 medium diamonds
   24 light diamonds
   118 medium 3″ triangles
   75 light 3″ triangles
   18 background hexagons from a 5″ strip
   12 background flat pyramids from a 2¾″ strip at 5¼″ on the Clearview Triangle
   32 triangle halves from 3½″ strip of background fabric

2. Make 20 of block A and 12 of block B.

3. Make 20 of strip A and 15 of strip B. Assemble 4 of row A and 3 of row B, ending the rows with the correct top and bottom partial blocks.

4. Seam rows together alternately according to the quilt diagram. To complete the pattern, add the left border strip of background flat pyramids, medium diamonds, and light triangles, and add the right border strip of background flat pyramids, dark diamonds, and light triangles. Add additional borders as desired. Elizabeth Sevy used border strips measuring 4½″ dark, 1¼″ medium, and 2″ light (outside to inside-measurements include seam allowance).

Piecing Diagram

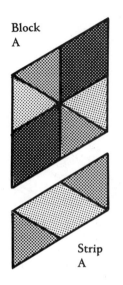
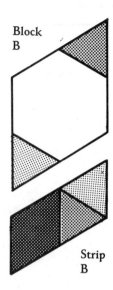

Block A   Block B

Strip A   Strip B

Partial Blocks

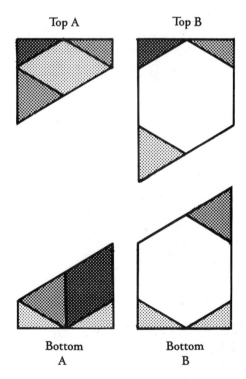

Top A   Top B

Bottom A   Bottom B

Trellis

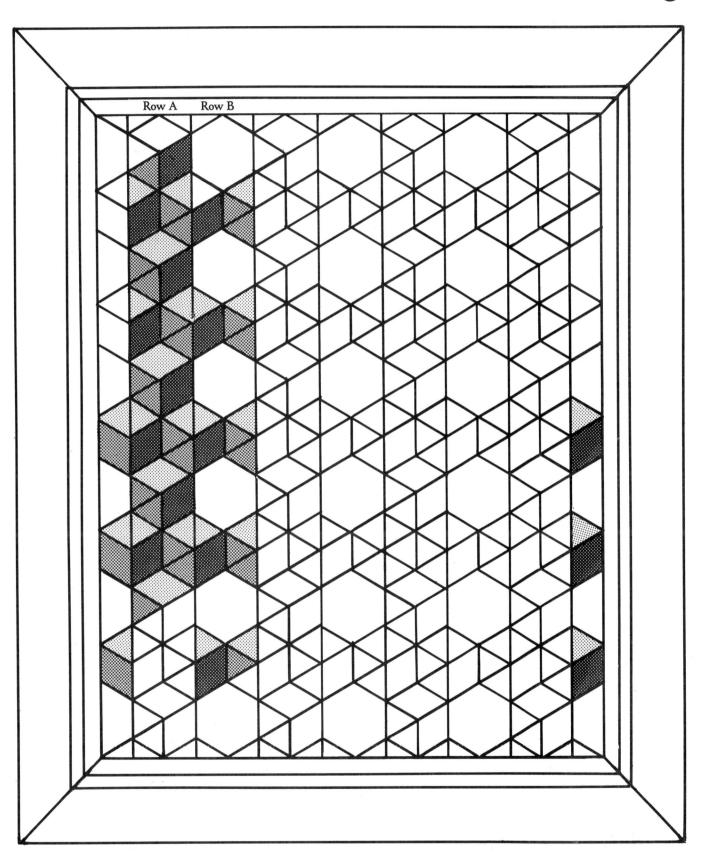

Row A   Row B

3 Blocks

3″ triangle

Quilt with borders:
56½″×73″

Fabric requirements for
quilt without borders:
1½ yd. dark fabric
1½ yd. medium fabric
1½ yd. light fabric
2 yds. background fabric

Directions:

Cut for 1 block:
3 dark diamonds from 2¾″ strip
3 medium diamonds from 2¾″ strip
2 background diamonds from 2¾″ strip
6 light 3″ triangles
2 background 3″ triangles
1 background flat pyramid from 2¾″ strip
    cut at 5¼″ on the Clearview Triangle
1 background flat pyramid from 2¾″ strip
    cut at 7½″ on the Clearview Triangle

1. Piece each block in rows as shown. Make 23 complete blocks.

2. Piece 2 partial top blocks. Cut for each:
light, medium, and dark pieces same as for complete blocks above
2 background diamonds
1 background 3″ triangle
2 background flat pyramids cut at 5¼″ on the Clearview Triangle
4 background triangle halves cut from 3½″ triangles
Assemble in rows as shown.

3. Piece 2 partial bottom blocks. Cut for each:
    light, medium, and dark pieces same as for complete blocks above
    1 background diamond
    1 background 3″ triangle
    1 background flat pyramid cut at 7½″ on the Clearview Triangle
    4 background triangle halves cut from 3½″ triangles
Assemble in rows as shown.

4. Assemble quilt in rows A+B according to the quilt diagram. To achieve various color effects behind the dimensional blocks, plan the background colors block by block, laying out the blocks on the floor or pinning them to a quilt wall as you proceed.

5. Cut 10″ strip of background fabric. Cut end to a 60° angle as shown. Sew to top or bottom of Row A. Cut off, leaving extra fabric to be trimmed later. Do this 5 more times.

6. Sew rows together. Trim edges. Laura chose an inner border of 2¼″ triangles, adding a 2″ strip of fabric at ends. Corners are mitred. Add a 4½″ outer border.

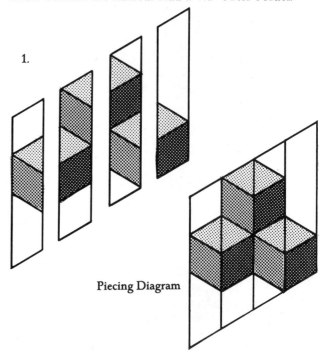

1.

Piecing Diagram

Partial blocks

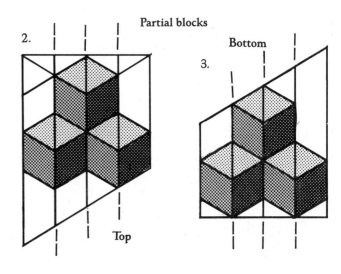

2.

Top

Bottom

3.

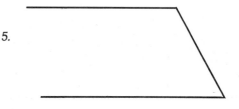

5.

3 Blocks

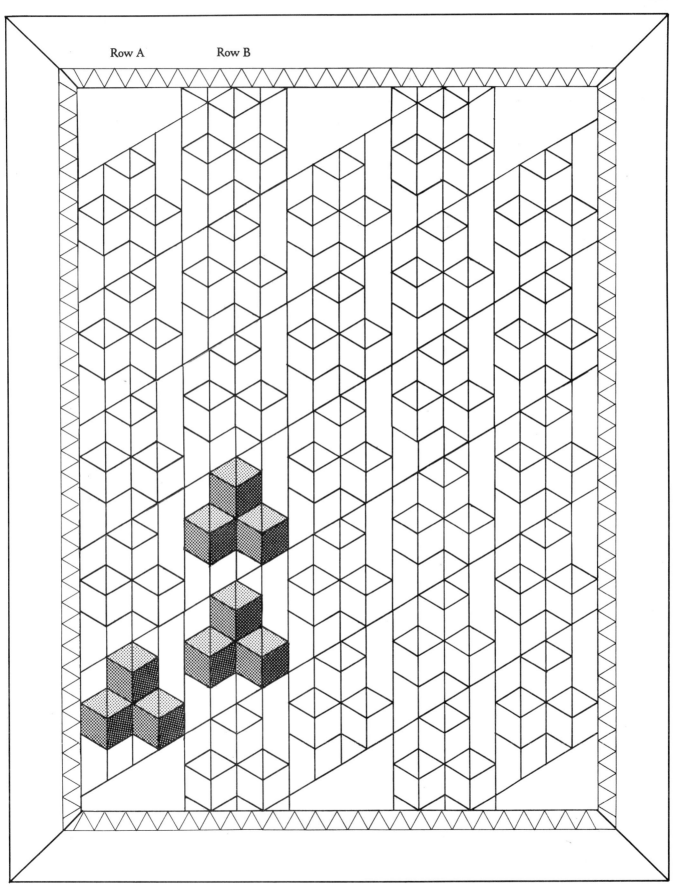

Row A   Row B

Miami Condo

7″ triangle

Technique: strip piecing

Quilt with borders:
60½″ x 78″

Strata #1

strip 1	3¼″ black fabric
strip 2	3½″ colored fabric
strip 3	1¼″ white fabric

Strata #2

strip 1	3¼″ dark gray fabric
strip 2	3½″ tan or silver
strip 3	1¼″ white fabric

Fabric requirements:

1½ yds. muslin
2⅓ yds. black
1¼ yds. dark gray
⅔ yd. silver-gray
1 yd. tan
½ yd. light blue
⅓ yd. royal blue
⅓ yd. light turquoise
⅔ yd. navy blue
⅓ yd. pink
⅓ yd. light olive
¼ yd. gold or bright yellow
⅓ yd. reddish brown

Directions:

1. Construct both strata (sets of strips). Press. Cut 7″ triangles from the strata. Use only the white-based triangles in the quilt. The others are set aside for another project of your choice.

2. Sew white-based triangles into attic window blocks and arrange into 2 sections as shown in the diagram. (A narrow section includes the silver and tan windows and the larger panel is composed of the vari-colored windows.)

3. Add 7″ triangles to each section to form the top of the building. Then sew the sections together, adding shapes to finish the top and bottom. Finish with a 1″ border of black fabric and a 5″ muslin border.

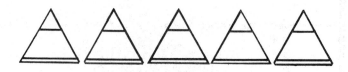

Triangles with white strip on base

One block

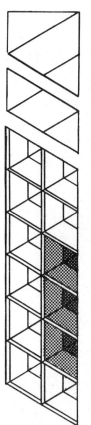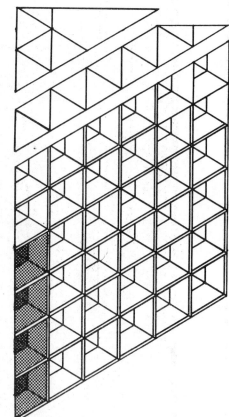

Two sections

Miami Condo

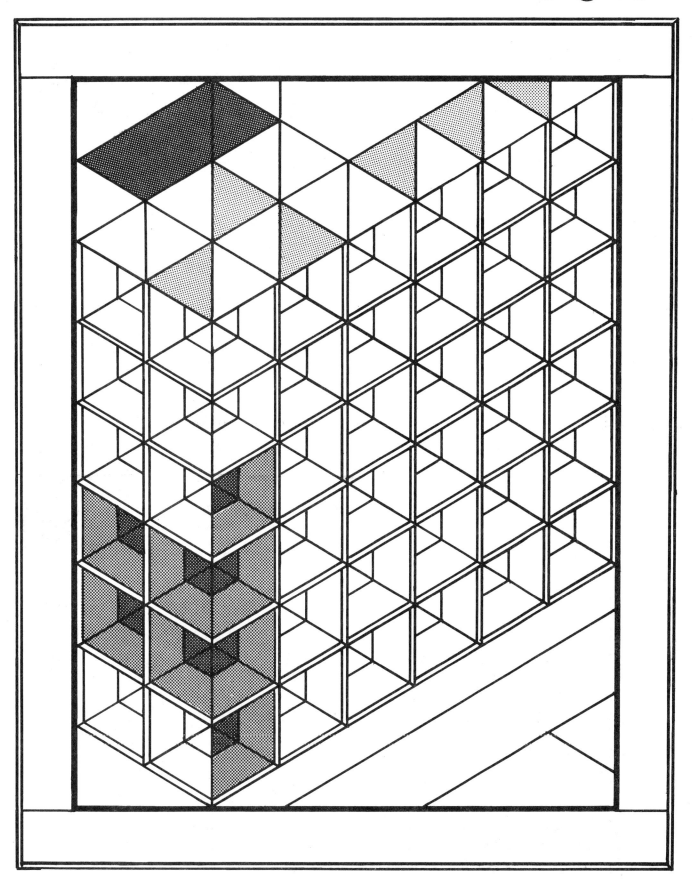

Winchester Cathedral

2½″ triangle

Quilt with borders:
65½″ x 76½″

Fabric requirements:

⅓ yd. each of 6 different dark fabrics
⅓ yd. each of 6 different medium fabrics
⅓ yd. each of 6 different light fabrics
1½ yd. background fabric
1½ yd. medium border fabric

2 similar blocks are used for quilt

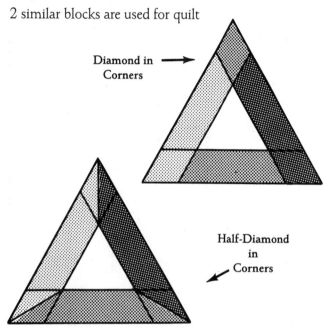

Diamond in Corners →

Half-Diamond in ← Corners

Directions:

1. Cut:
78 background 4¼″ triangles
78 light flat pyramids from 2¼″ strip at 6″ on the
    Clearview Triangle–42 white and 38 light blue
78 dark flat pyramids at 6″–42 black and 38 dark blue
78 medium flat pyramids at 6″–42 red and
    38 medium blue
36 light blue diamonds from 2¼″ strip
36 medium blue diamonds
36 dark blue diamonds
126 half-diamonds from 1⅝″ strip
    (make 3 value combinations
        light-dark
        light-medium
        medium-dark)
    make 3 sets of strips of each combination, then
    make more half-diamonds later if needed
12 background 9¾″ triangle halves

To piece one block:

1. Seam the medium pyramid to the medium triangle as shown.

2. Make a strip from the white pyramid and a light-medium half-diamond.

3. Make a strip from the dark pyramid, the dark-light half-diamond, and the dark-medium half-diamond.

4. Sew strip #2 and strip #3 to triangle #1 in order. Make 41 more of these.

5. Assemble 36 blue blocks in the same manner, using diamonds instead of half-diamonds.

6. Assemble into 6 rows of 13 blocks each, finishing the top and bottom of each row with a 9¾″ triangle half. Arrange the blocks to best advantage, being sure to keep them properly oriented as to shading. Sew the rows together.

7. Add a 7″ strip of medium fabric to the top and bottom of the quilt. Then add right and left pieced borders made from 4¼″ triangles and flat pyramids cut from a 4″ strip at 9¼″ on the Clearview Triangle. Last, to left and right sew a 3″ strip of medium fabric.

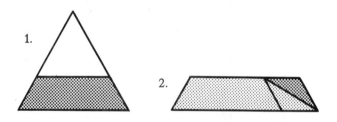

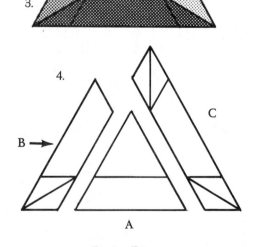

Piecing Diagram

Winchester Cathedral

Paintbox...a Quilters Colorwheel

by Charisa Martin Anderson

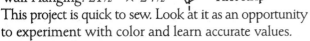
1" excess

Second strip

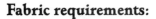
First strip

3¾" triangle

Wall Hanging: 21½" × 24½"

This project is quick to sew. Look at it as an opportunity to experiment with color and learn accurate values.

Fabric requirements:

small amounts of scraps (6"×20") of each color or:
¼ yd. each dark, medium and light of red, yellow, blue, orange, purple and green

background: ¼ yd. black print with white figure (dark)
¼ yd. black and white print (medium)
¼ yd. white print with black figure (light)

Directions:

Secondary-colored boxes
    (orange, purple and green)

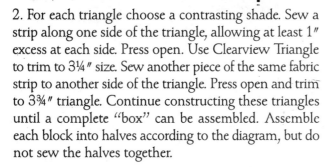

1. For each color box cut:
2 dark 2¾" triangles
2 medium 2¾" triangles
2 light 2¾" triangles
1 dark strip 1"×20"
1 medium strip 1"×20"
1 light strip 1"×20"

2. For each triangle choose a contrasting shade. Sew a strip along one side of the triangle, allowing at least 1" excess at each side. Press open. Use Clearview Triangle to trim to 3¼" size. Sew another piece of the same fabric strip to another side of the triangle. Press open and trim to 3¾" triangle. Continue constructing these triangles until a complete "box" can be assembled. Assemble each block into halves according to the diagram, but do not sew the halves together.

Primary-colored boxes

Red box

3. Cut:
1 dark 1¾" triangle
1 medium 1¾" triangle
2 light 1¾" triangles
1 dark 3¾" triangle
1 medium 3¾" triangle
1 dark strip 1½" × 20"
1 medium strip 1½" × 20"

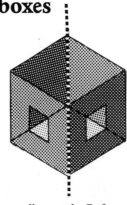

4. Sew a strip on 2 sides of each small triangle. Refer to diagram for value placement. Assemble block into halves.

Yellow box

5. Cut:
1 dark 1¾" triangle
2 medium 1¾" triangles
1 light 1¾" triangle
1 dark 3¾" triangle
1 light 3¾" triangle
1 dark strip 1½" × 20"
1 light strip 1½" × 20"

6. Sew a strip on 2 sides of each small triangle. Refer to diagram for value placement. Assemble block into halves.

Blue box

7. Cut:
2 dark 1¾" triangles
1 medium 1¾" triangle
1 light 1¾" triangle
1 medium 3¾" triangle
1 light 3¾" triangle
1 medium strip 1½" × 20"
1 light strip 1½" × 20"

8. Sew a strip on 2 sides of each small triangle. Refer to diagram for value placement. Assemble each block into halves.

Background and Final Assembly

9. Cut:
24 dark 3¾" background triangles
16 medium 3¾" background triangles
22 light 3¾" background triangles
6 medium 3¾" triangles, one in each primary and secondary color

Amounts are approximate. Use a variety of blacks to greys. Lay out in rows including the assembled half-blocks. Place the medium color wheel in the center according to the diagram. Evaluate the background values by squinting, use of a reducing glass, etc. When the arrangement is pleasing, seam the triangles and half-blocks together into vertical strips. Sew the vertical strips together. Press.

10. Trim design at top and bottom. Be sure to leave at least ¼" seam allowance. Check for right angles at corner using a wide ruler, T-square, etc. After machine quilting, Charisa added a multicolored binding.

Paintbox

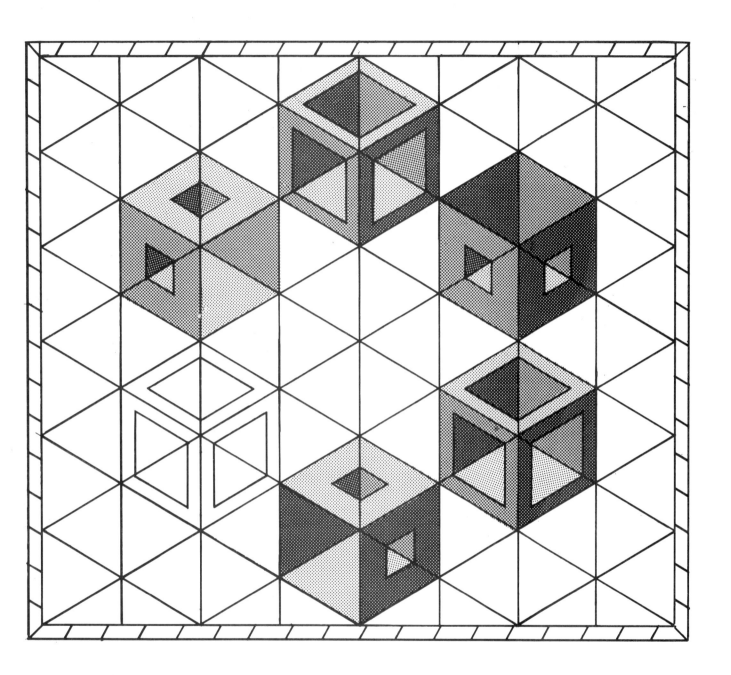

The Block Building

5¼″ triangle

Quilt size with borders: 47½″ × 64″

Fabric requirements:

1½ yd. dark fabric—can be
   3 different darks
1½ yd. medium fabric—can
   be 3 different mediums
1½ yd. light fabric—can be
   3 different lights
1 yd. background fabric
1¼ yd. outer border fabric

Directions:

1. Cut for quilt:

  32 medium 5¼″ triangles
  12 background 5¼″ triangles
  7 light 5¼″ triangles
  3 dark 5¼″ triangles

(cut these first,
then get the diamonds
out of the strip
leftovers)

  2 background triangle
    halves from 5¾″ triangle
  1 medium triangle half
    from 5¾″ triangle
  4 dark triangle halves from
    5¾″ triangle
  5 light triangle halves from
    5¾″ triangle
  13 medium diamonds from
    5″ strip
  2 light diamonds from 5″
    strip
  2 dark diamonds from 5″
    strip

Piecing Window Walls

2. Cut one 1¼″ strip of medium fabric selvage to selvage. Divide into 6 equal sections. Trim one end of each to a 60° angle as shown.

Cut one 1″ strip of dark fabric selvage to selvage. Divide into 6 equal sections. Trim one end of each to a 60° angle as shown.

4. Adding strips in the proper position to form a continuous 60° line along one edge, alternate the 1¼″ strip with the 1″ strip 6x.

5. Trim the 60° edge to be exact if necessary. Then, continuing to cut at a 60° angle, (use the Clearview Triangle itself or combined with a straight ruler) cut four 1¼″ strips from this strata. Be sure to cut the point in the direction shown.

6. Cut a 1″ strip of dark fabric. Trim one end to 60° angle as shown. Sew down the middle of 2 window strips resulting from #5. Finish top edge of windows with another trimmed 1″ strip.

7. From the same dark fabric, cut one 1¾″ strip. Trim one end to a 60° angle as shown. Sew to one side of a window strip. Trim the other end. Do the same thing on the other side of the window strip. Make another one of these. This completes 2 dark window-walls in one dark-medium combination. Eight more are needed, possibly in different color combinations.

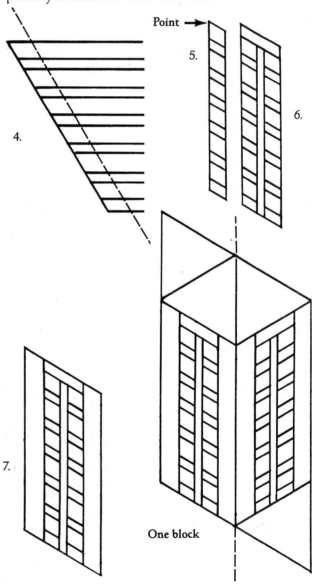

One block

Note: Laura pieced this from a planned color chart. Another and simpler approach would be to make blocks from the fabrics chosen—possibly scraps in dark, medium, and light—and then arrange the blocks as desired for final assembly.

8. The light-dark window walls are constructed in the same way, but when following instructions #2-7 change the medium strips to dark and the dark strips to light. Also, **very important,** in directions #2-7 cut all 60° angles in the reverse directions.

Compare the angle you cut with the diagram for either the dark or light window side of the building.

9. Assemble 8 complete blocks, using for each:
3 medium 5¼" triangles
1 background 5¼" triangle
one dark window wall
one light window wall
Construct 2 partial blocks, substituting a triangle half for the 5¼" background triangle in the top partial block and for the 5¼" medium triangle in the bottom partial block.

10. Construct a center horizontal row from 4 blocks. Construct a top and bottom row using 2 complete blocks and either a top or bottom partial block in each. Finish the top and bottom row with fill-in pieces as shown.

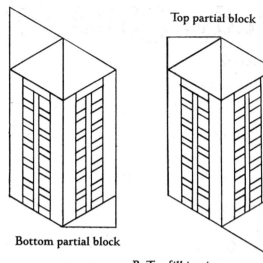

Top partial block

Bottom partial block

B. Top fill-in piece

B. Bottom fill-in piece

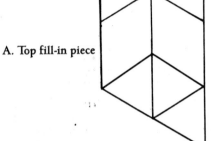
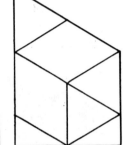

A. Top fill-in piece

A. Bottom fill-in piece

A. Top Fill-in Piece

1 dark triangle half from 5¾" triangle
1 light triangle half from 5¾" triangle
1 dark diamond from 5" strip
1 light diamond from 5" strip
1 dark 5¼" triangle
1 light 5¼" triangle
1 medium 5¼" triangle
(all these are already cut)

A. Bottom Fill-in Piece

1 dark triangle half from 5¾" triangle
1 light triangle half from 5¾" triangle
2 light 5¼" triangles
1 dark diamond from 5" strip
1 medium diamond from 5" strip
1 background 5¼" triangle
(all these are already cut)

11. Sew these 3 rows together.

12. Finish bottom left and top right to rectangle with remaining fill-in pieces B. Finish with desired borders.

B. Top Fill-in Piece

2 dark triangle halves from 5¾" triangle
2 light triangle halves from 5¾" triangle
1 medium triangle half from 5¾" triangle
2 dark 5¼" triangles
2 light 5¼" triangles
2 medium 5¼" triangles
1 dark diamond cut from a 5" strip
1 light diamond cut from a 5" strip
(all these pieces are already cut)
2 background 5¼" triangles

B. Bottom Fill-in Piece

2 light triangle halves from 5¾" triangle
2 dark triangle halves from 5¾" triangle
1 background triangle half from 5¾" triangle
2 light 5¼" triangles
1 dark diamond from 5" strip
2 medium diamonds from 5" strip
(all these pieces are already cut)

Laura used the scraps left from making the windows for a 2" striped inner border, and added a 4½" wide outer border.

Study: Child's Play

3″ triangle

Quilt with border:
58½″ x 71¼″

22 different blocks

When using prints, cut long diamonds with points up or down as indicated. (See cutting directions pg. 11.)

Directions:

Piece the assortment of blocks desired according to the individual directions given below. Arrange blocks into rows of 2, 3, or more blocks each. The number of rows will depend on the desired dimensions of the finished quilt. Finish each row with background triangle halves cut from a 10¼″ × 6″ rectangle as shown. Add 9¼″ × 6″ fabric pieces to the ends of alternate rows as in diagram. Trim edge as necessary. A strip of background fabric can be used to offset some blocks in order to add interest to the composition. I added a 7″ light gray border (includes seam allowance).

Fabric requirements:

I chose from 8 packets of hand-dyed fabric. Each contained approximately 1 yard in ⅛ yd. swatches, graduated shades of the same color. The colors were sorted by value and each block built separately. Additional fabric was used in the background and borders.

OR: 1½ yd. various dark fabrics
     1½ yd. medium fabrics
     1½ yd. light fabrics
     3½ yds. background fabrics
Border: 2¼ yds. light gray

Choose the blocks you like and repeat them or not to make a quilt or wall hanging whichever size you prefer.

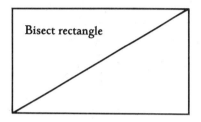

Bisect rectangle

A. Cut:

2 background triangles cut at 5¼″ on the Clearview Triangle
2 dark triangles cut as above
1 medium diamond cut from 5″ strip
1 light diamond cut at 5″
Assemble according to diagram.

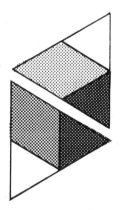

B. Cut:

4 background 3″ triangles
2 background flat pyramids cut from a 2¾″ strip at 9¾″ on the Clearview Triangle
2 dark flat pyramids cut at 5¼″
1 medium long diamond cut at 5″
1 light long diamond at 5″
Assemble according to diagram.

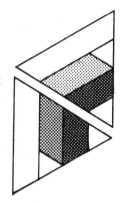

C. Cut:

2 background triangles cut at 5¼″ on the Clearview Triangle
2 background 3″ triangles
1 background diamond
1 light diamond
2 dark flat pyramids cut at 5¼″
1 medium diamond from 5″ strip
1 light long diamond at 5″
Assemble according to diagram.

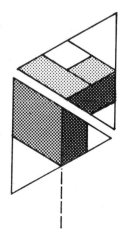

D. Cut:

2 background triangles at 5¼″ on the Clearview Triangle
2 medium triangles at 5¼″
1 light long diamond at 5″
1 dark long diamond at 5″
1 background long diamond at 5″
1 light diamond
1 dark 3″ triangle
1 background 3″ triangle
Assemble according to diagram.

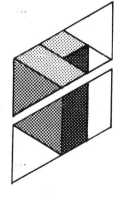

E. Cut:
2 background triangles cut at 5¼″
on the Clearview Triangle
1 background diamond from a 5″
strip
4 background 3″ triangles
2 medium 3″ triangles
2 dark 3″ triangles
2 light diamonds
1 dark diamond
1 medium diamond
Assemble according to diagram.

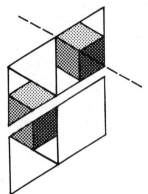

F. Cut:
2 background 5¼″ triangles
2 background diamonds
2 medium 3″ triangles
2 light 3″ triangles
2 dark flat pyramids at 5¼″ on the
Clearview Triangle
1 medium long diamond at 5″
1 light long diamond at 5″
2 dark 3″ triangles
Assemble according to diagram.

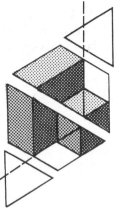

G. Cut:
2 background 3″ triangles
2 dark flat pyramids at 5¼″ on the
Clearview Triangle
1 light long diamond at 5″
1 medium long diamond at 5″
2 background triangles at 5¼″
2 background diamonds
1 light diamond
1 medium diamond
Assemble according to diagram.

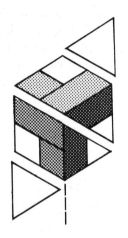

H. Cut:
2 background triangles cut at 5¼″
on the Clearview Triangle
2 background 3″ triangles
2 background diamonds
3 medium diamonds
3 light diamonds
6 dark 3″ triangles
Assemble in rows.

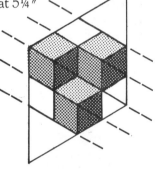

I. Cut:
4 background 3″ triangles
3 light 3″ triangles
2 dark 3″ triangles
1 background long diamond cut at 5″
1 dark long diamond cut at 5″
1 medium long diamond cut at 5″
2 medium diamonds
1 light diamond
1 dark diamond
1 light flat pyramid cut at 5¼″
Assemble according to diagram.

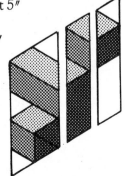

J. Cut:
2 background long diamonds cut
at 5″ on the Clearview Triangle
1 dark long diamond cut at 5″
2 dark diamonds
3 medium diamonds
1 background diamond
2 background 3″ triangles
6 light 3″ triangles
Assemble in rows.

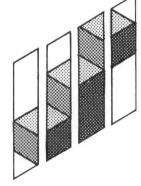

K. Cut:
3 background 3″ triangles
3 dark 3″ triangles
1 background 5¼″ triangle
1 medium diamond cut from a 5″ strip
1 background flat pyramid cut at 5¼″
1 dark flat pyramid at 5¼″
1 light long diamond at 5″
1 medium diamond
1 light diamond
Assemble according to diagram.

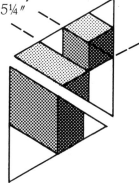

L. Cut:
2 dark 5¼″ triangles
1 medium long diamond at 5″
1 light long diamond at 5″
2 background flat pyramids cut at 9¾″
2 background 3″ triangles
Assemble according to diagram.

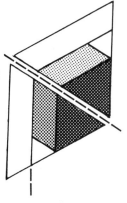

M. Cut:
Same as H
Assemble in rows.

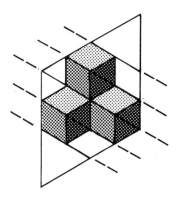

N. Cut:
2 background 7½″ triangles
4 background diamonds
1 light diamond
1 medium diamond
2 dark 3″ triangles
Assemble 2 halves, seam across middle.

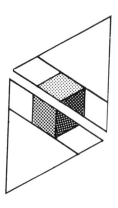

O. Cut:
1 dark 3″ triangle
2 background triangles
4 light triangles
1 medium diamond
1 dark diamond
1 dark flat pyramid at 5¼″
2 background flat pyramids at 5¼″
1 medium long diamond at 5″
1 background long diamond at 5″
1 background 5¼″ triangle
Assemble into 2 halves according to diagram.
Seam across the middle.

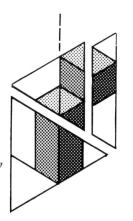

P. Cut:
1 dark diamond cut from 5″ strip
1 background 5¼″ triangle
1 light 5¼″ triangle
2 light 3″ triangles
1 medium 3″ triangle
1 medium long diamond cut from 2¾″ strip at 5″
1 background 3″ triangle
1 background 2¾″ strip–cut to the proper angle –sew on and trim.

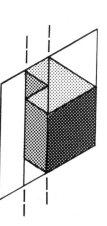

Q. Cut:
1 dark diamond from 5″ strip
1 dark diamond
1 light diamond
2 medium diamonds
4 background 3″ triangles
2 dark 3″ triangles
2 light 3″ triangles
1 light long diamond at 5″
1 medium 3″ triangle
1 medium flat pyramid at 5¼″
Assemble according to diagram.

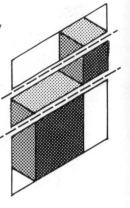

R. Cut:
2 background long diamonds at 5″
1 light long diamond
2 background 3″ triangles
3 medium 3″ triangles
1 medium flat pyramid at 5¼″
1 light diamond
1 dark diamond
1 dark diamond cut from 5″ strip.
Assemble according to diagram.

S. Cut:
2 light 3″ triangles
2 dark 3″ triangles
1 background diamond
1 medium diamond
2 background flat pyramids at 5¼″
2 medium flat pyramids at 5¼″
1 light long diamond at 5″
1 dark long diamond reversed
1 background 5¼″ triangle
Assemble according to diagram.

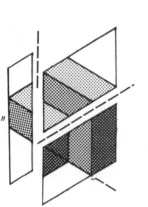

T. Cut:
3 dark diamonds
3 medium diamonds
2 background diamonds
2 background long diamonds at 5″
6 light 3″ triangles
2 background 3″ triangles
Assemble in rows.

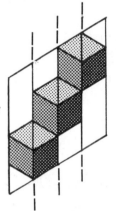

U. Cut:
4 dark diamonds
4 medium diamonds
8 background 3″ triangles
8 light 3″ triangles
Assemble according to diagram.

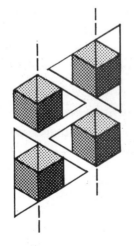

V. Cut:
1 background 5¼″ triangle
1 medium 5¼″ triangle
1 dark diamond from 5″ strip
1 background 2¾″ strip cut to the proper angle–sew on and trim
1 light long diamond at 5″ on the Clearview Triangle
2 medium 3″ triangles
1 light and 1 background 3″ triangle
Assemble in rows.

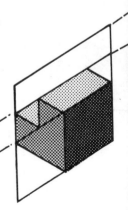

Study: Child's Play

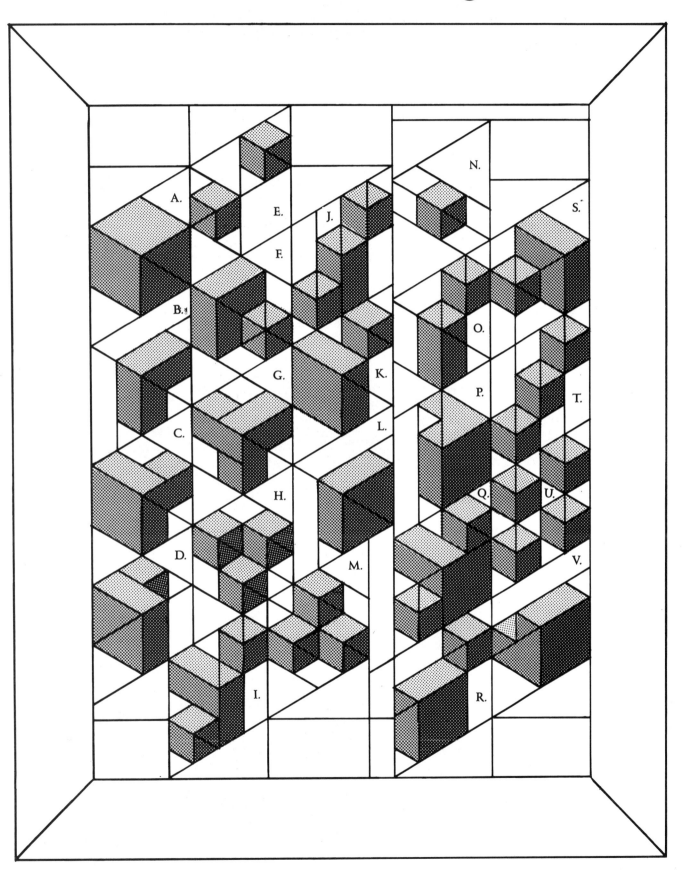

For the Designer

General Rules for Successful Designing

1. **Do it for fun**. Quilters experimenting with designs are like children playing. We learn while we enjoy ourselves. The most difficult designing is when we have to "play" by someone else's rules (called "custom" work) as when a quilt is requested in a certain pattern and particular colors. The easiest is when we are excited by a new technique or approach and can hardly wait to try it. The following suggestions can help keep designing fun:

Have the right tools: colored pencils or pens, fine white paper or graph paper, erasers, scissors and glue, good light and a comfortable chair or lap board.

Be sure to plan some free time for designing and dedicate it to yourself.

Eliminate distractions. This may mean satisfying your conscience with a clean house, taking that disco music off the stereo, or not trying to design at the beach.

2. **Never stop with one design**. Continue designing as long as you enjoy the process or as long as your time allows. Then put your work down and pick it up again tomorrow or next week. Try to put on paper all the possibilities that occur to you, and look for more. Go over past or rejected designs and look for ideas that can be reworked into another complete design.

3. **Choose one design**. Select a final design after laying out and reviewing all your completed sketches. Be sure you have on paper all the possibilities that occur to you. Usually there is one design that appeals to you much more strongly than any other.

4. **Evaluate and perfect the final design**. Tape the sketch on a wall so it can surprise you as you come home from work or are cleaning house. Leave it up for several days or weeks. If some part of the design is irritating, boring, etc., this will gradually make itself known. Draw a correction, tape it in the proper place in the design, and view this version for a while.

Another technique is to hold the design up to a mirror. This method can also reveal weaknesses and strengths. It's better to let yourself see design flaws before they have been sewed into fabric.

5. **Continue to learn**. Designs will improve if you follow your inner promptings and continue to experiment in various directions. The quilter can learn basic art principles through classes, books or workshops given by visiting artists. Entering work in exhibits or contests may be a harsh brush with reality, but if we are brave we can benefit from allowing others to offer opinions of our work.

Getting the design on paper

Graph paper makes getting your design on paper easy. You can simply color a grid rather than having to sketch the whole thing. Many designs can be shaded in just dark and light, leaving color choices to be made in the fabric store.

I like to use black fine and wide lined markers to completely fill in the little triangles or squares of the graph paper. Red is distracting and blue doesn't copy well. (You may want to shrink a part or all of the design or produce it in multiples for a repeat. The copy machine is a useful tool for working with dark-light designs.)

Some designs, however, need to be worked out in color. Again, I prefer to completely fill in the little squares or triangles of the graph paper as the sections of the quilt will be filled with particular fabrics. If you want a light hue, fill it lightly but completely. For color design work, I prefer colored pencils to colored pens because they are closer to fabric colors. Also, an eraser will often remove colored pencil in order to substitute a different color. Scissors and glue or double sticky tape are handy for corrections, too. Just cut out another colored or white section of graph paper and stick it in place.

When I go to the fabric store, I try to match the design colors as closely as possible. Most important, however, is to have the values of the fabrics match the values of the various parts of the design.

To design 3-D quilts, outline shapes on equilateral graph paper, divide into planes using connecting lines (see pg. 6) and shade these planes light, medium and dark (sometimes there's a background also).

Limiting the area to be dealt with sometimes makes the project easier. Instead of staring at a full blank page, choose a small section of grid and try to put 3-D shapes in that. For example, *Study: Child's Play,* shown on pg. 31, is made from 22 different blocks. I began by choosing a small diamond-shaped area of grid, 4 rows high and 4 rows wide. Then I tried to see how many different shapes and combinations I could fit into this small grid, stopping at 22 so the quilt wouldn't get too big.

Piecing an Original Design

When the design satisfies you, it is necessary to plan the seams that will be sewn. It is always possible to piece equilateral designs as a series of triangles. But many larger shapes can be cut in one piece, thus eliminating seams. However, my choice is usually to do easy machine piecing with all straight seams, so sometimes shapes **do** have to be cut up. It's good to stay alert for a repeat unit, or block, that would have the ease of traditional piecing. The choice of seaming will affect the finished appearance of the design (compare STRIP CITY and HANGING GARDENS OF BABYLON), so consider all the possibilities. Then determine the size of your quilt by choosing the basic triangle size, and begin cutting and piecing according to the rules and methods described in this book.

Calculating Fabric Requirements for an Original Design

Once triangle size is decided, the rules and tables given in this book make it easy to determine how many yards of each fabric are needed. Every shape is cut from a certain width strip. Estimate how many of each shape can be cut from each strip, then divide that number into the total number of each shape needed. You will then know how many strips in this width you will need. Multiply the number of strips by the width in inches, divide by 36″ to determine number of yards, and round to the next larger quarter or half yard to allow for shrinkage. Add a bit more if you really like the color.

Planning a Quilting Design

Many people find choosing a pattern to quilt a difficult part of the design process. To emphasize the 3-D effect in a quilt, a pattern that follows the lines of the shape is often the best choice rather than a more random quilting pattern. Stitch-in-the-ditch or a grid pattern have been effective for me. A background, however, can have strong curves to contrast with the angles of the foreground cubes and corners.

If a complicated original pattern needs to be quilted, try placing the graph paper design inside a clear plastic page protector, securing it with a couple of pieces of tape. Then tape another stiff piece of clear plastic over the folder. Draw the quilting pattern on the attached top sheet, using a permanent marker with a narrow tip. Devise a quilting pattern that will complement the design of your quilt. If you make mistakes, replace the plastic sheet and draw the pattern again, correcting as necessary until you are satisfied. Leave the quilting pattern taped over the quilt design and use it as a guide for marking the quilt all at once, or a hoopful at a time.

Bibliography

Diehl, Gaston. *Vasarely.* New York: Crown Publishers, Inc., 1973.

Fairfield, Helen. *Patchwork from Mosaics.* London: B.T. Batsford, Ltd., 1985.

Locher, J.L., ed. *The World of M.C. Escher.* New York: Harry N. Abrams, Inc., Publishers, 1971.

Fisher, Laura. *Quilts of Illusion.* New Jersey: The Main Street Press, 1988.

Gutcheon, Jeffrey. *Diamond Patchwork.* New York: Alchemy Press, 1980.

Locke, John. *Isometric Perspective Designs and How to Create Them.* New York: Dover Publications, Inc., 1981.

Paré, E.G., Loving, R.O., Hill, I.L. *Descriptive Geometry.* New York: The Macmillan Company, 1959.

Turner, Harry. *Triad Optical Illusions and How to Design Them.* New York: Dover Publications, Inc., 1978.

Willson. *Mosaic and Tesselated Patterns: How to Create Them.* New York: Dover Publications, Inc., 1983.

Index

About the Author

Sara Nephew began her artistry in metalwork. After receiving her B.A. as an Art Major, she worked for a commercial shop, repairing and designing jewelry, and invented a new enamel-on-brass technique. Her cloisonne' work appeared in national exhibits.

She has since turned her interests to quilting, in large part because of the many attractions of fabric. Sara is the originator of a series of tools for rotary cutting isometric shapes, and a nationally known teacher. She is the author of three previous quilting books. *Quilts from a Different Angle* was an introduction to 60° triangle quilts. *My Mother's Quilts: Designs from the Thirties* helped inspire renewed interest in depression-era quilts. And *Stars and Flowers: Three-Sided Patchwork* showed how to speed piece 60° quilts with a floral applique appearance.

Sara lives in Snohomish, Washington, with her husband Dale and their three children.

THE TOOLS used in this book are:

60° 6″ Clearview Triangle — ruled every ¼″	$6.50 plus $1.50 shipping*
60° 12″ Clearview Triangle — ruled every ¼″	$11.50 plus $2.00 shipping*
60° 8″ Mini-Pro — ruled every ⅛″	$ 9.50 plus $1.75 shipping*
120° Half-Diamond — ruled every ⅛″	$10.50 plus $2.00 shipping*
Graph paper...⅜ grid, ⅞ grid, or mixed packet—20 sheets	$ 3.50 plus $1.00 shipping*

Also available from Clearview Triangle:

Stars and Flowers: Three-sided Patchwork $12.95 plus $2.00 shipping*

* *Subtract $1.00 from shipping for each item after the first.*

ORDER FROM: Clearview Triangle
Dept. 4
8311 180th St. S.E.
Snohomish, WA 98290